"*The Couple Skills Workbook* is your road map to nurturing healthier relationships. Delve into your past and childhood, and gain insight into your physiological and psychological states to acquire invaluable tools for enriching your life and strengthening your bond. This guide fosters self-discovery and mutual understanding, paving the way for a fulfilling journey of healing and growth together."

—**Anna Aslanian, LMFT**, founder and director of My Therapy Corner, certified trauma and couples therapy specialist, supervisor, and consultant in California

"Betsy Chung's *The Couple Skills Workbook* is the workbook I wish I had when I started my marriage. Full of practical ideas, powerful insights, and helpful exercises, this book is a valuable resource to help you get to know yourself and your partner better, as well as provide you with tools to build a healthy and deeply intimate relationship."

—**Leah Katz, PhD**, clinical psychologist, and author of *Gutsy*

"Written with wisdom, depth, authenticity, compassion, and clarity, Betsy Chung provides pragmatic tips for healing, communicating, and thriving in relationships. Self-compassion is a prerequisite for healing and providing compassion to our partners, and readers will learn both. A must-read for all couples."

—**Sue Varma, MD**, psychiatrist, and author of *Practical Optimism*

"*The Couple Skills Workbook* is a practical and thorough guide that will be incredibly helpful for couples who need to strengthen their emotional connection, communication skills, and individual emotional regulation. As a couples therapist, I will recommend it to my clients and use it myself. It is well paced and covers all the critical components of relational intelligence. Indeed, it is a gem."

—**Kim Swales, PhD**, relationship expert, researcher, counselor, and host of the *Connecting with Dr. Kim Swales* podcast

"If you're looking to develop your connection with your partner, *The Couple Skills Workbook* is for you. Betsy Chung has written a compassionate, practical, and comprehensive guide to improving your relationship. With her guidance, you'll learn how to understand and respect each other's needs, and acquire invaluable tools for effective communication and conflict resolution. This is an indispensable resource for any couple seeking to strengthen their bond."

—**Catherine Topham Sly**, BACP-accredited couples therapist, relationship transformation coach, and creator of the Love Happy Live Free personal development and relationship skills training program

"This book speaks to the heart of couples who have felt relational stress, emotional distance, or uncertainty in their relationship. Not only does the author provide practical tools and engaging activities, but she also guides with her own vulnerability, understanding, and therapeutic insight. An essential guide that teaches you how to empower your empathy, strengthen your relationship, and understand your blind spots when resolving conflict."

—**Nabill Zafir**, licensed mental health counselor

The Couple Skills WORKBOOK

Manage Conflict,
Increase Trust & Intimacy
& Build a Better Relationship

Betsy Chung, PsyD

New Harbinger Publications, Inc.

Publisher's Note

This publication is designed to provide accurate and authoritative information in regard to the subject matter covered. It is sold with the understanding that the publisher is not engaged in rendering psychological, financial, legal, or other professional services. If expert assistance or counseling is needed, the services of a competent professional should be sought.

NEW HARBINGER PUBLICATIONS is a registered trademark of New Harbinger Publications, Inc.

NATIONAL CENTER FOR NCEO MEMBER EMPLOYEE OWNERSHIP

New Harbinger Publications is an employee-owned company.

New Harbinger Publications, Inc.
5720 Shattuck Avenue
Oakland, CA 94609
www.newharbinger.com

Cover design by Sara Christian

Acquired by Ryan Buresh

Edited by Karen Schader

Printed in the United States of America

26 25 24

10 9 8 7 6 5 4 3 2 1 First Printing

To my husband, Antonio, for showing me what security feels like.
To my mom and dad for showing me that marriages can be fun.

Contents

Part 3: Applying Relationship Skills

Introduction

Love is perhaps one of the most enigmatic concepts of the human experience. Everybody is eager to find love, but few understand what it takes to build relationships that are healthy and fulfilling.

Relationships are a necessary part of our healthy functioning and have the potential to enrich our lives and lessen our burdens, but they can also be the source of much turmoil and distress if not approached with intention.

Particularly during stressful times, without good understanding of the causes behind our uncomfortable feelings, we may inadvertently respond in ways counterproductive to our larger goal of preserving connection, leading to frustration and uncertainty about the relationship's future.

But just because humans share a common need for social connection doesn't mean that we're all equipped with the proper tools to sustain healthy relationships. Having deep affection for somebody is not enough to foster a good partnership. In fact, without tools to understand and address our emotions in a healthy manner, that deep affection can be the very thing that destroys our most valued relationships.

It's important to understand that the relationship we have with our partners is not simply another feature in our lives. Rather, it becomes part of the infrastructure that supports a good life, so we must learn to take care of each other because our partner's comfort has a direct effect on ours. For two people to be truly fulfilled in a relationship, both must feel that their needs are being addressed, which can be a complicated task because we all have our own unique life stories that affect our values, perspectives, and expectations. This is why one of the biggest obstacles that couples face in sustaining long-term happiness comes from not knowing how to manage interpersonal differences.

When it comes to creating a life with another person, disagreements are to be expected rather than feared as signs of incompatibility, and learning to navigate differences has to be accepted as part of the relationship-building journey. No relationship is immune to problems, so instead of feeling burdened by them, you can learn to use them as building blocks to strengthen your partnership.

Attaining relationship security isn't as intuitive as one would hope, thanks to our society's habit of placing higher value on securing physical safety over emotional safety. Most of us are much more capable of explaining why we shouldn't touch a hot stove with our bare hands than articulating to somebody how we feel, leaving us frequently dissatisfied because we don't know how to effectively convey what we need to feel better.

Because humans are social animals by nature, *functional* relationships are essential for survival. What this means is that simply having people in our lives is not enough—relationships need to be balanced and meaningful, which can be difficult to achieve without some level of *relationship IQ*.

Relationship IQ (RQ) can be conceptualized as a byproduct of a more familiar concept—emotional IQ (EQ). A person with high EQ is confident in the management of their emotions because they understand why they feel the way they feel, and trust in their personal resources to resolve personal difficulties and restore their inner peace. Similarly, a person with good RQ is confident in their management of interpersonal relationships and has tools to maintain relationship equilibrium by balancing their personal needs with consideration for others.

While some people are more inclined toward healthy relating, it's not an innate skill. In fact, those who have higher RQ were usually raised by caregivers who were emotionally competent and who *also* benefited from caregivers with good relational skills. What this means is that RQ is nurtured, and therefore just about anybody can learn to have good relationships.

Through many years of research, observing, and analyzing relationships, I believe I've uncovered some of the answers to maintaining lasting, fulfilling relationships—including my own. Some people might be tempted to assume that because I know a lot about relationships, that must mean I have an easy or even "perfect" relationship. But no amount of expertise can protect any relationship from the inevitable clashes that will arise whenever you attempt to mash two individual lifestyles into one. If anything, my greatest revelations have come from picking apart my own relationship challenges in order to make better sense of what works, what doesn't work, and why. Over time, I turned my insights into effective relationship tools that I've shared with my private psychotherapy clients to help them connect deeply with their partners. Each time my clients said things like "You hit the nail in the head" or "I tried the thing we worked on and the result was much better," it reinforced the value that I place on my relationship philosophies. And now I want to share them with you so that you too can find satisfaction in your relationships.

But before we get into all of that, I'd like to set some expectations. First, you must know that the skills I teach you and your partner will not come naturally. Consider your chronological age, and that's how old your existing relationship habits are, so patience is key because old habits die hard, and new ones take time to integrate. Particularly in the beginning, many of these practices may feel forced and cause you to question why you're giving up your existing relationship dynamics for ones that feel artificial. But remember that *change* is precisely why the two of you have decided to embark on this journey, and you can expect parts of it to be uncomfortable.

Second, the aim of this workbook is not to help you and your partner develop a conflict-free relationship or to save marriages. After completing this book, you and your partner will still argue, you may continue to make mistakes that result in hurting the other person, and you'll experience the occasional bouts of disconnect because both of you are human with human emotions. But rather than letting challenges destroy your relationship, I'll teach you how to use them to deepen your intimacy with each other.

This workbook is most appropriate for couples who generally get along well but have difficulty navigating setbacks. For example, maybe you genuinely value your partner as a great person but want more passion in the relationship. Maybe you've been considering couples counseling but want to try something less intensive. Perhaps the relationship feels unbalanced, you worry that you and your partner are too different, or you wish you felt more sure about the relationship.

Through carefully crafted exercises, you'll both become aware of the patterns that interfere with your relationship intimacy, be able to articulate and understand each other's needs better, and increase your RQ by learning effective tools for approaching problems with more direction. Without the right tools, it might be easy to feel discouraged by your ability to navigate common relationship hurdles, causing you to misinterpret periods of stuckness or disconnection as signs that the relationship is failing and beyond help.

I believe that relationships are resilient and are rarely beyond help as long as both partners are motivated. However, self-guided healing work, such as this workbook provides, will always have limitations. Human psychology can be extremely complicated, and the contents of this book are not adequate to address severe trauma or mental illness, and are not appropriate for relationships involving any form of abuse. If you believe that your relationship struggles could be associated with your mental or emotional health, and/or you are victim to sexual/mental/emotional/physical abuse, immediate help is available to you here:

National Domestic Violence Hotline
800-799-7233

Substance Abuse and Mental Health Services Administration (SAMHSA)
800-662-HELP (4357)

Throughout my life, I've witnessed deserving individuals tragically end relationships with each other because they couldn't figure out how to effectively communicate, connect, and work through conflicts together. But as I dove deeper into my research, whether by reading books, working with private clients, or observing my own relationship interactions, it became clear to me that there are methods to make love last in a healthy and fulfilling way. By the time you complete this workbook, my hope is that you'll feel closer to each other, feel more assured about the partner you chose, and have faith in your partnership's ability to overcome whatever hardships you may be confronted with.

How to Use This Book

This book is designed to be used by two people who are mutually invested in strengthening their relationship intimacy through development of healthy relationship tools. To do this, you must (1) gain a basic understanding of what healthy relationships entail and (2) build fundamental tools to effectively navigate relationship interactions.

This workbook will take you on a three-part journey that begins with learning about yourself through basic education about human emotions and relationship needs, and developing awareness of your own internal processes that can affect how you relate to others. Although this book is primarily focused on romantic relationships, the relationship skills you learn could be extremely effective when applied to other types of relationships as well.

In part 2, you'll dive deep into the mechanics behind healthy relationships and develop relevant tools to boost your relationship IQ (RQ) in order to connect with your partner on a more profound level. As you move through the first two parts of the workbook, you'll find skill development exercises as well as suggestions for practice between sessions in order to help deepen your understanding and application of concepts. Finally, in part 3, you'll learn how to apply the tools you learned in parts 1 and 2 to enhance common relationship interactions and work through conflicts with purpose.

Most of the exercises in this workbook will require participation from both of you in playing the role of either the *practicing partner* or the supporting partner. When you complete an exercise, you'll swap roles and repeat the exercise so you both have a chance to practice the skills.

The practicing partner takes a more active role in sharing personal experiences and practicing skills, while the supporting partner will be the guide through the exercises by reading prompts aloud and writing down responses when instructed to. Though it may seem like the supporting partner's job is simple, it's actually an essential part of the work. As supporting partner, you'll passively develop listening skills by following suggestions on how to be supportive and listen with intent. These suggestions are in italics. As you move through the book, you'll continue to internalize more tools that you'll gradually incorporate into your supporting role as not just a facilitator of exercises but also an emotionally supportive partner.

To further organize the process, you'll each be identified as either *Partner A* or *Partner B* for the entirety of the workbook. For each exercise, try to change which of you goes first, making sure that you each get an opportunity to practice and develop every skill.

Occasionally, there will be exercises that call for your own self-reflection, so I recommend that each of you keep a personal journal where you can jot down thoughts or insights. You can use a notebook or an existing journal, or simply staple pieces of scratch paper together. While writing space is provided for most exercises, many discussion topics are sensitive in nature, and you may not feel ready to share everything with your partner. Although part of the goal of this workbook is to be able to be authentic and vulnerable, you should also have agency over your private thoughts and feelings. Therefore, know that you are the final person who should make the decision about what, when, and how much to share with your partner.

Now you know the way exercises will be structured, so for your first task, decide which of you will be *Partner A*, and which will be *Partner B* for the remainder of this book. Write down your decision here:

*Partner A:*____________________________________

*Partner B:*____________________________________

Whether you're the initiator of this journey or you agreed to come along for the ride, the message is clear: both of you are invested in the longevity of this relationship. Like any other commitment, consistency is key, so if feasible, I recommend that you dedicate about one to two hours of uninterrupted time weekly to work on this book together. See this as a deliberate effort to set aside time for each other. You can even make a date out of it!

To get the most out of this book, give yourselves time to digest and apply the concepts and tools covered, rather than muscling through. To help, you'll find recommended pauses along with suggestions on things you both can do to continue the work outside of your sessions. However, if there's ever a time that you feel uncomfortable or resistant to continuing, you can cut workbook sessions shorter. I highly advise *against* jumping ahead in chapters or doing more than recommended in one sitting.

To keep you accountable and gauge your progress, each time you return to the workbook, you'll be asked to check in with each other, engaging in a guided discussion about things you've learned or noticed about each other, what you're doing well, and things to improve on. Questions in these discussions are intended to help you and your partner develop productive conversational skills, and your responses do not need to be written down.

On the next page, you'll find a blank worksheet titled Relationship Toolbox. Bookmark this page as you'll be asked to refer back to it often. This is where you'll record the wins you've reflected on during your weekly check-ins. The main purpose of having this toolbox is for the two of you to build confidence in your partnership by recognizing your strengths as a couple, and to have accessible tools for immediate reference in case the two of you need reminders to get past challenges.

Relationship Toolbox

Throughout the book, if it ever feels like either of you are struggling to grasp certain concepts, don't hesitate to review or even repeat previous chapters. The deeper your understanding of the content, the more resources you have to engage healthily with your partner.

Take a moment right now to discuss and agree to a routine that works well for the two of you. Keep in mind that a same day, same time each week may not be realistic for everybody, so you can choose to play it by ear, to schedule two weeks at a time, or to follow whatever plan will work best for you.

In the space provided, write down the plan you've agreed on:

*We agree to work on this workbook with the following routine:*____________________

____

____

____

You may have experienced some resistance to committing to a routine. Not only is that okay, it's also normal. Each time you add or change something in your life, you're being asked to disrupt a routine that's generally worked for you. Whether you're giving up a gym routine or time to scroll social media after dinner, new commitments are emotionally laborious.

Right now, I'd like both of you to take a moment to share what you're giving up to accommodate this work and tend to your relationship. Write it down and share it out loud with your partner. If you can, explain the importance behind your sacrifice. For example, giving up an hour of TV time may actually mean giving up the hour you need to wind down after a busy workday.

*Partner A:*____________________________________

____

____

*Partner B:*____________________________________

____

____

Now that you've heard what your partner is giving up for you, I'd like each of you, in the order you choose, to take a moment to show your partner gratitude for their efforts by reading aloud the following sentence, inserting your own word(s) in place of the blank lines:

Thank you for giving up_______________in order to do this with me. I understand that it's been an important part of your routine because it provides you with_______________. The fact that you're willing to make accommodations for me makes me feel_______________.

After you've both offered gratitude to each other, take a minute or two to digest what your partner just said to you, and try to notice if it shifted anything within you. Go ahead and do it now before moving on…

The purpose of this last exercise was to start the two of you off on good footing by instilling some internal motivation, not to just work on this book but to continually seek a connection with each other. What makes appreciation such a great motivator is that it makes the receiver feel as though the things they do are being seen and adding value to the relationship. If you take the time to notice, there are countless things that you and your partner do every day to support your relationship, but when those small efforts are overlooked, continuing to do them can feel meaningless. Showing appreciation for each other can stimulate positive feelings about the relationship and make you and your partner feel valued. There's more to be discussed in later chapters about the effects of appreciation, but you don't need to understand it to reap the benefits of it.

Time for a Pause

Though it may not seem like it, the two of you have already achieved a lot by committing to a new regimen for the shared purpose of elevating your relationship. This might be a good place for the two of you to pause. In the coming weeks, expect to be introduced to heavier content, which will be much more manageable if you're both feeling good about the relationship. This is why your only homework this week is to prep your relationship for the challenging yet rewarding work that's to come.

You can start by actively looking for opportunities to appreciate your partner during your break:

- Notice the things your partner does that make your life significantly easier, and make that known to them.
- Think about what your partner's life was like before you entered it, and acknowledge the things they've given up for the relationship.
- Pay attention to your routine together and notice the kind of teamwork that goes into it.
- Share these things with your partner.

Pay attention to the different ways your partner contributes to your relationship, share what you notice with them, and you'll see how doing so little can do so much to elevate your relationship.

Checking In

Welcome back! By the time you're reading this, at least a couple of days should have passed since you were last here. After many of the breaks suggested in this workbook, you'll return to a guided discussion similar to the one you're about to engage in. The goal is to keep both of you accountable because the only way you'll get anything out of this book is to actively apply what we talk about in here to interactions with your partner.

You were both asked to pay attention to things you appreciated about each other. Engage each other in a discussion by taking turns responding to the questions that follow. Be thoughtful about your responses, but don't spend too much time on them. This discussion should not take longer than ten minutes of your time.

On a scale of 1 (dissatisfied) to 5 (very satisfied), how do you rate your relationship interactions since your last workbook session?

You were asked to pay attention to different ways your partner contributes to the relationship. What are the contributions you most appreciate, and how do they benefit the relationship?

What are things your partner already does to show appreciation?

What are things you do to show appreciation to your partner?

What's something you can do better for your relationship this week?

Getting to Know Yourself

As a psychologist who specializes in helping individuals achieve healthy relationships, I hear a lot of amateur theories about what it takes to be happy in a relationship. Some people say it's about the right timing, others might seek money or status, and among the most common theory I hear is compatibility. While I'm not going to entirely deny that there's some value in those attributes to make a relationship work well, my experience has pointed to something else—emotional competence.

A big problem many people have in maintaining functional relationships is that they don't know how to control the intense emotions that get stirred up when they get close to somebody. Without proper management, those emotions create obstacles to intimate connection and weaken even the seemingly strongest of relationship bonds over time.

But before we learn to manage our relationships with *others*, we must first gain understanding of how we relate to *ourselves*, which is what the first three chapters of this book are dedicated to.

In chapter 1, you'll learn all about a built-in need that *all* humans have, and what it has to do with relationships. Then, in chapters 2 and 3, we will go deeper and give you a better sense of what emotions are, how they drive our behaviors, and how to deal with them. Let's jump in.

CHAPTER 1

Understanding Your Need for Emotional Security

Security is a sense of safety that transcends the present. It comes from trusting that you have adequate resources to deal with whatever adversities you may encounter. In other words, when you feel secure, you believe that no challenge is ever going to be too great for you to endure.

There are many types of security. For example, some pursue financial wealth because having a lot of money will secure the means to take care of their physical needs for a lifetime. Others may work extra hard to outperform coworkers because it gives them the feeling that their job is secure. And while money and professional accolades provide some stability in certain aspects of our lives, neither is enough to satisfy our primal need for *emotional security*.

Emotional security is different from other types of security because it cannot be manufactured or measured; rather, it's an internal state that comes from trusting that you have the emotional capacity to cope with stressful circumstances. A person who is emotionally secure still experiences the full range of human emotions, like anger and anxiety, but rarely allows those emotions to get the best of them because they know that they're capable of finding solutions, whether through self-management, having access to reliable, supportive relationships they can lean on when things become too overwhelming, or both. Ultimately, this means that emotional security cannot be achieved without also having secure relationships. Although the two are distinct forms of security, one cannot exist without the other, so from this point on, I will use the terms "emotional security" and "relationship security" interchangeably.

At our core, humans are social animals and are innately wired for interpersonal connection. In other words, relationships not only improve our quality of life but also are part of our biology and therefore necessary for us to thrive. Particularly during infancy, we need human connection. Because babies are reliant on caregivers to meet all of their life-sustaining needs, their sense of security greatly depends on the quality of their caregiver relationship.

For young children to feel fully secure, they need to trust that their caregivers are committed to being there to relieve both their physical and emotional discomforts. This commitment is crucial to a developing child because they are otherwise incapable of tending to their own needs.

Those raised in warm and loving environments are familiar with feeling secure, and therefore generally have healthy standards for relationships throughout life. The affection they received from their caregivers demonstrated that closeness was a positive experience, which can later translate to healthy intimacy in adult relationships. In adulthood, they tend to experience more overall satisfaction, be more likely to select partners who make them feel secure, and have acquired healthy relational tools from their caregivers to effectively manage relationships.

Unfortunately, not all children are raised by caregivers who understand the full range of their developmental needs. Many caregivers tend to be better versed in meeting their children's basic needs for food and shelter than their emotional needs. Typically, these caregivers were emotionally stunted themselves because *they* weren't taught to effectively deal with emotions, whether it be their own or others', leaving the children also emotionally impaired.

These children often felt insecure and unloved, not because their caregivers didn't love them, but because their caregivers failed to show love in a way that *felt* like love. To feel loved, children need to know that their caregivers are committed to their well-being under *any* condition—the good, the bad, and the messiness of growing up. This doesn't mean that your caregivers should have showered you with love even when you misbehaved, but you trusted that they were still devoted to you even when you disappointed them.

Emotionally unavailable caregivers are not necessarily bad or abusive. Most of the time, they're very well-intentioned but fail to recognize how their actions or expectations could affect their emotionally underdeveloped children.

Take a mother who punishes her young daughter with silent treatment after a disagreement, causing her daughter to worry whether the two would ever speak again. Consider a jaded father who intends to prepare his son for the harsh realities of the real world by telling him "Boys don't cry," causing the child to believe that he should always suppress and conceal his real emotions. Think about an anxious caregiver who scolds their six-year-old for hurting their knee after falling off a tree, causing the child to feel as though they were doing something bad by exploring their environment.

In all of these examples, there's a hidden message from the caregiver to their child—there are conditions to be met if the two are to have a good relationship. Though they seem mild on the surface, repeated experiences like these can cause a child to stress about their lovability and feel as though they need to work hard to preserve closeness with their caregiver. These children usually grow to become adults who continue to question their value to their partners, and struggle to find a sense of security in their relationships unless they meet certain conditions.

The truth is, emotionally available or not, most caregivers are devoted to their children and would be there for them under just about *any* condition. But if that wasn't clear to you during childhood, it makes sense that you would find tension with loved ones a threat to your quality of life.

Here's a list of common caregiver–child interactions that may cause a child to feel insecure about their bond with their caregiver. Review the list out loud with your partner, and write your identification letter (*A* or *B*) next to those experiences that remind you of your relationship with your primary caregiver.

- Criticized you when you made mistakes
- Compared you to others
- Spanked you
- Gave you the silent treatment
- Shamed you for doing things poorly
- Embarrassed you in front of others
- Lectured you frequently
- Was upset by your crying
- Called you overly sensitive
- Punished you frequently
- Was always too busy for you
- Was difficult to please
- Expected you to care for your siblings

- Expected your siblings to care for you
- Said no all the time
- Treated others better than they treated you
- Left you home all the time
- Was always irritable
- Made you feel incompetent
- Threatened to disown you
- Accused you of being bad
- Was suspicious of you
- Told you to go away
- Never did the things you wanted to
- Showed no interest in you or things you shared

The following questions for discussion pertain to the list the two of you just reviewed. Decide who will be the first supporting partner, and swap roles when the practicing partner has completed responding. *Supporting partner*, please read the following questions aloud and give your partner time to respond to each question.

Of all of the examples that you marked above, which reminded you most of your relationship with your caregiver?

Share with me an example of what that looked like.

What message did you take away about what's acceptable (or unacceptable) from such interactions?

How do you think that message shows up in our relationship?

Tell me about any other experiences with your early caregiver(s) that may have caused you to question their devotion to you.

What kind of message did you take away from that?

How do you think that message shows up in our relationship?

Time for a Pause

Let's pause here and give you some time to digest this important concept of emotional security. During your break, continue paying attention to things you appreciate about your partner, and begin the process of getting to know yourself on a deeper level by paying attention to the kinds of situations that cause you to feel insecure or question your partner's love for you. Specifically, make note of times when you feel as if you have to do certain things, or meet certain conditions to preserve your partner's love. To guide your practice, ask yourself these questions:

- What conditions do I believe must be met to be considered a good partner?
- What am I afraid will happen if I don't meet those conditions?
- Are these conditions a direct request from my partner or self-imposed?
- What's a more realistic expectation for myself?
- What can I do to support those more realistic expectations?

Checking In

Before the pause, you learned about what emotional security is, why it's so crucial to the human experience, and how various caregiver–child dynamics can disrupt a child's sense of security. To feel secure, children have a primitive need to feel that their caregivers love them unconditionally and will be there for them *no matter what*. Because they're so dependent on their caregivers to survive, children are extremely sensitive to signs of disconnection from their caregiver. Especially at a very young age, even the slightest sense that their caregiver is unhappy with them can be stressful and cause them to make desperate attempts to restore a positive bond. In the next chapter, you'll learn about how these stressful experiences can affect a developing child, and begin to uncover how your childhood relational experiences influence what you expect from and how you behave in your intimate adult relationships.

Check in with each other by engaging in a guided discussion, taking turns responding out loud to the questions below. Be thoughtful about your responses, but also don't spend too much time on them. This discussion shouldn't take longer than ten minutes.

On a scale of 1 (dissatisfied) to 5 (very satisfied), how do you rate your relationship interactions since the last time you worked in this book?

What did the two of you do well together this week? If you consider this a strength of your relationship, write it down in your Relationship Toolbox.

Share with your partner a moment this week where you felt obligated to do something you didn't want to do.

What would you have preferred to do instead in that moment?

Are these expectations self-imposed, or were they specifically requested by your partner?

What are you afraid would happen if you chose not to follow through with the expectation?

Did you notice or learn anything new about your partner this week? If so, what?

Did you notice or learn anything new about yourself this week? If so, what?

What's something you can do better for your relationship this week?

CHAPTER 2

Breaking Down Your Childhood Defenses

To understand your present emotional struggles, you must first have some basic knowledge about the hidden forces that drive them. Every human is born equipped with a nervous system, an internal mechanism that continuously works behind the scenes to keep us alive, and helps us interact with the world around us. Without your nervous system to relay information from your external surroundings to your inner processes, you'd be at the mercy of your environment and would succumb to your surroundings. For example, if not for your nervous system, you wouldn't know what to do about a bear charging full force toward you.

What gives you the will and energy to take action against threat are the involuntary processes of your nervous system, which consists of your brain, your spinal cord, and a network of millions of nerves that span your body. Your nerve endings sense information from your immediate environment and passes it through your brain. Your brain processes the information, makes meaning out of it, and assigns it an emotion.

An emotion is an involuntary reaction to some meaningful event, and its purpose is to inform you of how to react. While emotions can produce physical feelings, they're more than merely bodily sensations; they must also be preceded by some subjective perception of the event—in other words, a personal story that explains what happened. Each time something meaningful happens to you, whether good or bad, your brain will capture significant details of the experience, including how you felt, what you were thinking, and how you responded, and will create a story about it that gets stored into memory.

Depending on the type of emotion, one of two subdivisions of your nervous system is activated, each containing different hormones that are sent through nerve channels that direct your organs on how to behave.

If your brain appraises information as neutral or nonthreatening, it activates your *parasympathetic nervous system* (PNS), which releases hormones that have calming and restorative effects on your internal system. The main objective of the PNS is to keep you functional so that you can tend to your day-to-day, life-sustaining duties. In addition to regulating your bodily organs to ensure that your internal systems are in proper working order, your PNS processes and stores important information about meaningful events into memory so the information can be used to help navigate life.

On the other hand, if your brain perceives incoming stimuli to be stressful or threatening, then your *sympathetic nervous system* (SNS) becomes activated and releases energizing hormones to mobilize life-saving functions. Known as the fight-or-flight response, this system prepares your body to either run from or fight off real or perceived threats in the immediate environment by activating or suppressing certain organ functions to maximize your chance of survival. For instance, hormones released by the SNS will accelerate your heart rate to increase oxygen flow so you can run; dilate your pupils to give you a wider peripheral view of your surroundings; and suppress your reasoning abilities so you can maintain sharp focus on the threat. Physically, these effects cause you to feel restless and uncomfortable with a sense of urgency to take life-saving action. Because the fight-or-flight response only becomes activated under a state of stress, for the remainder of this book, each time I mention the word "stress," it should automatically be associated with the fight-or-flight response.

This all probably sounds pretty dramatic for the world we live in today. Though as adults we don't commonly encounter life-threatening circumstances that should warrant a fight-or-flight response, recall from our last chapter that children *are* constantly vulnerable to the dangers of the world because they're so defenseless. To children, any sense that their caregivers are unavailable to tend to their life-sustaining needs could be experienced as a life-threatening event.

Young children feel safest when they're intimately connected to those they're the most familiar with. Intimate connection is the degree of closeness between two people and doesn't refer only to romantic partnerships. Children raised by emotionally intelligent caregivers tend to feel secure because of how well their caregivers know them and how to meet their needs. This doesn't mean that high EQ caregivers never disappoint their children, but when that happens, they know how to restore their sense of safety. Children whose caregivers lack emotional competence, on the other hand, are less likely to have their needs met. They frequently feel insecure and are therefore more prone to stress-response activation. Not only are they rarely comforted when distressed, but they're not taught to appropriately express their needs in a way that others can easily comprehend.

The more intimacy you share, the more secure you'll feel because there's a higher chance that you know how to meet each other's needs. This following exercise will help the two of you gauge the present level of intimacy in your relationship.

Decide which role each of you play to start, and swap roles when completed.

Supporting partner, read aloud the following questions to your partner and write down their responses in the spaces provided.

On a scale of 1 to 5, how well do you think I know you?

*Partner A:*____________________

*Partner B:*____________________

Share something that you think I don't know about you.

*Partner A:*____

Partner B: ____

What's something I know about you that nobody else knows?

*Partner A:*____

*Partner B:*____

On a scale of 1 to 5, how well do you think you know me?

*Partner A:*__________________

*Partner B:*__________________

What's something that only you know about me?

*Partner A:*____

*Partner B:*____

What's something that makes our relationship unique?

*Partner A:*____

*Partner B:*____

Those who didn't feel as though their caregivers knew them intimately tend to have a hard time dealing with their emotions in productive ways. In childhood, when they were in distress and didn't have assistance from their caregiver to help them restore a sense of safety, they were left to their own devices and would use whatever limited resources they had to attempt to feel better. This might've looked like molding themselves to the standards of their caregivers to gain approval and avoid rejection, using aggression to discharge pent-up energy in the form of tantrums, or distancing themselves from the source of discomfort. Whatever seemed to resolve the emotional distress would've been stored as insight about how to handle similar occurrences in the future.

So if as a child you weren't taught how to manage difficult emotions, you would likely struggle as an adult to manage emotions that come up around interpersonal conflicts. When faced with uncomfortable situations, rather than working collaboratively with your partner to find reasonable solutions, you'll deal with them in the most familiar way you know, only slightly evolved.

Consider these examples:

- You were ignored when upset and needed to dramatize your feelings to get your caregiver's attention, so in your adult relationships, you cause dramatic scenes during arguments if you feel unheard.

- When you felt treated unfairly, arguing with your caregiver only made things worse, so you learned to never to advocate for yourself, even in your adult relationships.
- You frequently felt like you were disappointing your caregiver unless you were being "good" and obedient, so in adulthood, you suppress personal needs and cater to your partner to earn their favor.
- When somebody upset you, your caregivers fiercely defended you by condemning the wrongdoer, so you, too learned to vilify those who hurt you.

Patterns of insecure caregiver relationships during childhood tend to be repeated in adult romantic relationships due to the intimate nature of those relationships. Similar to a child's fear of losing connection with their caregiver, it can be particularly stressful when the relationship with our chosen partner isn't going well because the familiar life we created with them is threatened.

Though tension with loved ones never feels good for anybody, disagreements tend to be significantly more stressful for those who had insecure attachments while growing up. When there's tension between caregiver and child, deliberate efforts need to be made by the caregiver to restore the connection or else children are left to worry whether the caregiver bond will ever be recovered. For children of caregivers who fail to repair ruptures, the mere presence of conflict could activate a fight-or-flight response. In adulthood, this often results in an avoidance of conflict, which can inhibit the possibility of peaceful resolution of differences.

Though necessary for survival of emergency situations, an unmanaged stress response can interfere with your relationship in many ways because its natural function is to create distance; and yet you should always be seeking connection with your partner, particularly in times of turmoil. Furthermore, if *both* of you struggle to control your SNS reactions, then one person's stress response can easily trigger the other's defenses, resulting in an explosive back-and-forth that intensifies with each exchange.

While we all want to believe that we have personal agency over the things we do, the truth is that our fight-or-flight response activates involuntarily when it detects signs of danger, and if we don't learn to manage it, it can influence us to behave in thoughtless ways that can hurt our relationships.

Following a big fight, people often helplessly say things like "I don't know what came over me…" or "My partner just brings out the worst in me…" suggesting that they don't have any control over their responses. Although it may seem that way, we are very capable of controlling our reactions. Once we learn to manage our triggers, we *can* develop healthier ways to resolve our unmet needs.

Can you relate to this example?

Exhausted after a long day at work, Sienna returns home to unwashed dishes from the night before. She's immediately reminded of the way her family would leave dishes in the sink for her to wash, although she had two older siblings who could have done that chore. Believing that her partner, Sam, left the dishes for her to clean, Sienna accused him of refusing to help around the house. In response, Sam recounts all times that she left chores undone, which prompts Sienna to defend her contributions. A fight ensues.

Arguments like this are common, but they can be prevented. If Sienna recognizes that she's tired, perhaps she could be more mindful about her approach when asking Sam to help clean the dishes, or she could give herself a twenty-minute break after returning home before addressing the dishes.

Though useful for imminent, life-threatening emergencies, the fight-or-flight response tends to be more harmful than helpful to relationships. Depending on how conflict was handled during your childhood, even a simple disagreement can escalate into a full-on stress response. This is because your nervous system is designed to always seek comfort, and disagreements challenge what you already believe as truth. To effectively work through disagreements, you must learn to become aware of and manage your own signs of SNS arousal so you can create safe environments for both partners to openly share their feelings and needs. The following exercises will help you and your partner become aware of signs that your stress response is activated to help you better manage tense interactions.

Supporting partner, read these prompts out loud to your partner. Read slowly, and give your partner time to get comfortable.

Sit or lie down in a comfortable position.

Close your eyes and take a slow, deep breath in through your nose.

Exhale slowly through your mouth.

Keep breathing in this pattern, slowly in through your nose, filling your stomach with air, slowly out through your mouth.

Keep going.

(Give your partner time to settle in before moving on.)

Think of an upsetting experience that took place at any point in your life. Don't overthink. Just describe the first memory that comes up.

Partner A:____

____

____

Partner B:____

____

____

Take your time, and bring yourself back to that experience. Describe where in your body you feel any sensation as you're thinking about this experience. There could be many body parts affected. It's okay if you don't have perfect words for it. Try your best, take however much time you need, and tell me when you're done.

Partner A:____

Partner B:____

Thank you for sharing. Take whatever time you need to collect yourself, and open your eyes when ready.

Your fight-or-flight system has one job, which is to protect you from danger, so the relevant symptoms should cause you to feel uncomfortable and itching to take action. Many people complain of heaviness in their chest, muscle tension, shallow breathing, salivating, numb extremities, or sweaty palms.

But remember that when under duress, the SNS doesn't just activate certain organs, it also suppresses others. This means that you will not only experience changes in bodily sensations but will also have restricted access to certain functions. Of most relevance for us to talk about is the suppression of specific brain processes, such as controlling urges and seeing different sides to a situation.

There's good reason for this restricted access. During an encounter with danger, your organs must work very hard to maximize your chances at survival. In order to conserve energy, the SNS will shut down those internal functions that are least useful to crisis situations. For example, though careful weighing of options can be extremely beneficial to making big life decisions and future planning, contemplation can get you killed in an emergency situation. Under imminent threat, you'd be much better served if you were to follow your gut by taking quick, decisive actions.

Again, this is good for emergencies, but bad for relationships because when the SNS is activated, it suppresses the reasoning abilities of the PNS and quickly focuses all your attention on creating distance from the source of threat. Often this looks like combativeness, unwillingness to budge, or shutting down. Accompanying those behaviors are usually thoughts that support the behaviors. Similar to the way you learned to sense your physical signs of stress in the previous exercise, you can also learn to identify signs of SNS activation by becoming aware of the kind of thoughts that surface when under stress. In the following exercise, you will begin to identify your own stress-related thoughts. You'll both work on the exercise at the same time, and write down your responses on separate paper or in your personal journal. After you're both done, come back together to share your responses.

Below you will find several scenarios. You may choose to read them out loud together or privately to yourself, but the questions should be answered separately. As you go through each scenario, really try to imagine yourself in the situation.

Scenario #1

Your partner is picking up take-out from your favorite restaurant. You repeated several times that you didn't want any spiciness in your dish. When your partner returns with the food, you find your dish smothered in red chilis.

What do you feel?

What thoughts are going through your head?

What story are you telling yourself about the situation?

Scenario #2

You're bathing your four-year-old and realize there are no towels in the bathroom. You hear your partner laughing at a TV show and call out for them to bring a towel. Moments later, they storm into the bathroom, handing you the towel with a look of annoyance on their face.

What do you feel in that moment?

What thoughts are going through your head?

What story are you telling yourself about the situation?

Scenario #3

It's your best friend's wedding day, and you've been pressing your partner to start getting ready, explaining why it's important to show up on time. An hour later, you're ready to leave but your partner is not. You wait a little longer. The wedding is to start in forty-five minutes, the GPS says your trip will take forty minutes, and your partner is still not ready.

What do you feel in that moment?

What thoughts are going through your head?

What story are you telling yourself about the situation?

Next, think about a time where you became upset at your partner. Briefly write down what happened and answer these questions.

What did you feel?

What thoughts were going through your head?

What were you telling yourself about your partner's intention?

When you're in a state of stress, it's as though your entire being becomes hijacked, with your body and mind both purely focused on self-preservation. And though symptoms associated with SNS activation tend to be similar, not all stressful events will trigger the same symptoms, and not everybody experiences stress about the same things. This is because most of what we react to is the result of our *subjective* perception of things. For example, while many people find dogs adorable, somebody who was attacked by a dog during childhood might experience intense stress when they encounter other dogs in adulthood, and behave toward those dogs as if they were the ones who attacked them in childhood.

Similarly in relationships, negative relational experiences during childhood can influence how we approach relationships in adulthood. If nobody helped you make sense of upsetting relationship dynamics during childhood, you're likely to form your own stories about those experiences. Over time, those stories become part of your framework for how you should perceive and behave in relationships. Left unchecked, these self-narratives can lead you to misperceive your partner and their intentions, and fail to see who they authentically are.

You can learn to engage with your partner more authentically by identifying the kinds of faulty narratives you have about your interactions. It is my belief that a person who cares deeply for you will *never* intend to hurt you, so when you encounter situations where you feel hurt by your partner, that could be a perfect opportunity to investigate what story you might be telling yourself about who they are and what their intentions are.

Throughout this chapter, you should have picked up on the power of the SNS to influence how you behave in your closest relationships. Gaining awareness of your fight-or-flight response is to bring a previously unconscious drive into your consciousness so you can learn to manage its effects. Under stress-response activation you lose the capacity to reason, so problem resolution is only possible after you've restored a sense of safety and have access to the high-level brain processes regulated by your PNS, which will be discussed more in the next chapter.

From initial detection to reaction, your fight-or-flight process needs only a fraction of a millisecond to completely take over, which is what makes it impossible to prevent—and extremely difficult to control. Under tension with your partner, your fight-or-flight system will cause you to hyperfocus on self-protection, making it nearly impossible to work collaboratively. As a result, you may be more distrustful, argumentative, judgmental, and stubborn, which are all manners of relating that inhibit healthy problem solving. By becoming more aware of your SNS state and learning to manage it, you can clear the path for deeper connection with your partner.

Time for a Pause

Let's pause here and give you a chance to digest all the information you just learned. To continue the work during the pause, try and catch moments when you're stressed, and pay attention to your internal processes. What are you feeling? Where in your body are you feeling it? What does the dialogue in your head sound like under those states? I also challenge you to pay attention to your *partner's* signs of stress. Through the time you've been together, you and your partner have developed intuitions about each other. Whether or not you've been aware of it, you have the ability to sense when your partner is tense or relaxed. Until we meet again, you'll work on building confidence over your knowledge of your partner by doing the following:

- Observe your partner when they're stressed or upset. How can you tell by the way they look? The things they say?
- Pay attention to how you feel when your partner's stressed. What happens inside you? What's your internal dialogue in those moments? How does it cause you to behave?
- Try to pick up on certain situations that may trigger stress in your partner. Are there certain times of day? Certain topics that tend to upset them?
- Pay attention to the things that tend to help your partner calm down.

Checking In

Before the pause, you learned about your fight-or-flight system, how it affects you, and why it's important to get a handle on it. You guided each other through exercises to help you become aware of signs that you're under fight-or-flight activation and were asked over the week to pay attention to signs that your partner might be under a state of stress.

To check in, take turns responding to the questions below. Be thoughtful about your responses, but don't spend too much time on them. At the end of the check-in, you'll find several questions and instructions on how to respond.

On a scale of 1 (dissatisfied) to 5 (very satisfied), how do you rate your relationship interactions since the last time you worked in this book?

As a team, what do you do well together? If it feels like a strength of your relationship, write it down in your Relationship Toolbox.

As a team, what areas would you like to see improvement in?

Have you noticed any changes in your relationship—good or bad?

Did you notice or learn anything new about your partner this week? If so, what?

Did you notice or learn anything new about yourself this week? If so, what?

What's something you can do better for your relationship this week?

The following questions pertain to your assignment over the week to observe each other's signs of stress arousal. Your partner can be another valuable source of awareness to help you identify signs and manage your fight-or-flight symptoms. *Supporting partner*, read the following questions to your partner, and write down their responses in the space corresponding to their identifier (*Partner A* or *Partner B*). Swap roles when complete.

What's an example of a time when you knew I was stressed or in a bad mood?

*Partner A:*____

____

____

____

*Partner B:*____

____

____

____

What were the signs that told you I was in such a state?

*Partner A:*____

____

____

*Partner B:*____

____

____

What do you believe could have caused me to be in such a state?

Partner A:____

____

____

Partner B:____

____

____

How did you feel when I was in that state?

Partner A: ____

____

Partner B:____

____

What can I do to help you not feel that way?

Partner A:____

____

Partner B:____

____

CHAPTER 3

What Does Security Feel Like?

Now that you know what insecurity feels like, let's talk about what it's like to feel secure. Though you may not be consciously aware of the exact moments your fight-or-flight system becomes activated, when people are directed to pay attention, most can easily identify symptoms of their stress response. However, finding security is not quite as measurable because it's the end result of a long process.

What I mean by emotional security being a process is that it happens over time, and it is born out of an accumulation of experiences where safety is assured through successful management of personal hardships *and* the availability of others to depend on unconditionally.

Children raised in consistently warm and supportive family relationships, who were encouraged to explore and shielded from major life stressors tend to become emotionally secure adults because they experienced the world as a generally safe place. Knowing that they always had a trusted adult to turn to gave them the courage to learn about the world around them, take on healthy challenges, and develop personal strengths that would contribute to self-esteem. Though these children might not have been consciously aware of the security they had, they were comfortable enough so that they never had to want for anything more.

Though safety is required to feel secure, they're not the same thing. Safety refers to a present state of calm that is void of worry or danger and is dependent on your immediate surroundings, and security is a sense of trust that you'll be okay regardless of your immediate surroundings.

For example, let's say that your paycheck was late this month, and you were anxiously waiting for it so you could pay your mortgage. When the money was finally transferred into your account on the deadline for your mortgage payment, you felt safe for the rest of the month. However, what if you suddenly won a $10 million lottery prize? Knowing that you'd be able to cover every mortgage payment from here on out would give you financial security.

And though safety and security are not the same, safety is like a gatekeeper to achieving emotional security, so we cannot start looking for security without first knowing how to feel safe.

While your fight-or-flight response is associated with stress, safety is associated with comfort. Recall from the last chapter that your nervous system is constantly relaying information from your external environment, and directing your internal organs how to respond. If sensory information is appraised as potentially threatening, your brain activates your sympathetic nervous system (SNS), which causes you to feel urgency to take some sort of action. Without threat in the environment, your brain is reassured of safety and keeps your parasympathetic nervous system (PNS) in operation.

Your nervous system never sleeps, even when you're sleeping, so at all times you're either functioning under your SNS or your PNS. Ideally, we should be under a PNS state for the majority of our lives because the PNS is significantly more adaptive for sophisticated human life. Because humans have conscious awareness, we are able to do things that give us meaning, such as pursue personal growth and maintain meaningful relationships. In a safe environment where we don't have to be concerned about survival, we're able to benefit from all the calming features of the PNS and direct our attention toward enriching our lives.

The primary job of the PNS is to keep all of our organs working harmoniously. For example, you may be familiar with *homeostasis*, which is a feature of the PNS that helps regulate body temperature. When your body temperature drops, the PNS helps by sending signals throughout your body to shiver. When your body temperature rises too much, it'll send signals for your body to produce sweat to cool you down.

Other examples of the PNS's regulating processes include slowing the heart rate, maintaining a steady flow of oxygen, and relaxing the muscles, which all result in feelings of internal balance and relaxation.

Remember that in order to feel safe, you must be under PNS functioning, so let's take a look at what happens internally in the absence of a threat or danger. The following relaxation exercise will help you tune in to the bodily sensations associated with a sense of safety.

Decide your roles before you begin. Once you've completed the exercise, swap roles and do it again.

Supporting partner, guide your partner through this exercise. Once they're in a state of relaxation, you'll ask your partner a series of questions to help them connect to experiences where they felt safe. Take notes, but there's no need to write down everything verbatim. During the exercise, you'll be prompted to pay attention to your partner's posture, their facial expression, and any other signs that might suggest they're in a state of relaxation.

(Read slowly and take pauses where you feel appropriate to give your partner time to tune in to themselves.)

Get into a comfortable position... Close your eyes.

Place one hand on your stomach.

You're going to take a slow, deep inhale through your nose and fill your stomach with air as you breathe in.

You should feel the hand on your stomach rise as this happens.

At the top of your breath, hold it for one second before you slowly exhale a stream of air through your mouth.

(Notice any physiological changes in your partner.)

Take another slow deep inhale and fill your stomach with air...

Exhale slowly through your mouth...

Keep following that slow breathing pattern...

Do a quick scan of your body and see if there's any tension anywhere.

(What is your partner's facial expression like?)

Unclench your jaw...release your shoulders...let your arms go limp...

Keep breathing...

Think about a time when you felt very connected to somebody—it can be anybody—at any point in your life. Take your time, but don't overthink. Tell me when you have a memory in mind.

(Give your partner a moment to think.)

I want you to bring yourself back to that moment.

Set the stage for yourself. Where were you? Who was there? What happened?

(Give your partner a minute to settle into the memory.)

If you're comfortable sharing, tell me about it.

(Simply listen. Don't comment or provide any feedback. Continue when it feels right to.)

I'm going to ask you some questions about this experience. You might not have the perfect words to describe it; just try your best.

How did this person make you feel?

Partner A:______________________________

____

Partner B:______________________________

____

What were you feeling in your body?

Partner A:______________________________

____

Partner B:______________________________

____

Try to pinpoint the areas in your body where you felt those sensations.

Partner A:______________________________

____

Partner B:______________________________

____

What does this experience tell you about what you need to feel safe?

*Partner A:*____

____

____

*Partner B:*____

____

____

In addition to physical relaxation, under PNS functioning we have access to all parts of our brain, including the parts that get shut down when the SNS is activated; for our purposes, the *prefrontal cortex* (PFC) is the most important of these parts.

The PFC is the part of your brain that is responsible for high-level human cognition. In any given moment, your brain processes millions of pieces of sensory information, and the PFC helps you organize that information. For example, as you're reading this paragraph, your skin is sensing the temperature, and there's probably some passive background noise that you hear but are not focusing on, unless you choose to be.

Under a state of calm, because there's nothing urgent to tend to, you're at liberty to decide what to do with all the information in front of you. Let's say you promised your friend you'd attend their birthday bash, but the day of the party, you get tickets to a concert that you really wanted to go to. Assuming this isn't a life-or-death situation, you might weigh your options and try to find the best solution for you. Decision-making skills like this are important for living harmoniously with others. Because everybody is different, if the goal is to reap the benefits of interpersonal relationships, we must find ways to meet our own needs and at the same time consider the feelings of others. The PFC helps us do that.

So whether you're bonding or experiencing disagreements with your partner, chances of meaningful connection are significantly increased if you're both using the part of your brain that helps you consider each other's feelings. The following exercise will show you the type of thinking your PFC is capable of.

Decide which of you will go first. When all the questions have been answered, swap roles before moving on.

Supporting partner, guide your partner through the following relaxation exercise. Once they're in a state of relaxation, you'll ask your partner a series of questions about you and your relationship. Simply listen; there's no need to write their responses here.

(Read slowly and take pauses where you feel that your partner might need some time.)

Get into a comfortable position...close your eyes.

Take a slow, deep inhale through your nose, filling your stomach with air.

At the top of your breath, hold it for one second before you slowly exhale a stream of air through your mouth.

(Observe your partner. See if you can recognize when they're in a relaxed state.)

Take another slow deep inhale and fill your stomach with air...

Exhale slowly through your mouth...

Keep following that slow breathing pattern...

(Keep observing, and have your partner continue this breathing pattern until you can tell that they've relaxed.)

Now that you're in a relaxed state, I'm going to ask you some questions.

Think of any argument we had at some point in our relationship. When you have an example, please share.

How do you think I was feeling?

What do you understand about why I was feeling that way?

Rather than working on this workbook, if you could do anything at all, what would it be?

What's keeping you from doing exactly that?

If you had to choose between being filthy rich for doing a job you hated, or being middle-class doing a job you loved, which would you choose? Think out loud and share your thought process with me.

Here both of you were able to practice empathy by seeing a perspective other than your own, actively practice impulse control by not giving into temptations, and weigh pros and cons by exploring your values. All of these abilities (and then some) are crucial to the development of good relationship IQ (RQ), and are most available under PNS functioning.

However, as you've already read in the last chapter, some people who grew up experiencing a lot of worry about the strength of their caregiver bond are more prone to living under SNS activation. For some, minor issues such as picking a bad restaurant could activate a stress response that could shift the mood and ruin the meal. These people are so used to worrying about relationship bonds that they assume *any* imperfections can threaten their relationship, and therefore are frequently engaging in their relationships with limited access to the PFC. The result is difficulty being relaxed, open, and vulnerable around their partners.

The good news is that, although you don't have any ability to prevent activation of your SNS and PNS, there are tools you can use to bring the functions of your PNS back online—in other words, *coping skills*. A coping skill is anything you do to make yourself feel better in any given moment, and whether you know it or not, you already have a set of these skills. Let's find out what yours are.

On the following two pages you'll find two Coping Toolboxes, one for Partner A and one for Partner B. These are similar to the Relationship Toolbox, except you'll be using these to write down your *personal* coping skills. You may go in whatever order, but you should write down your own coping skills in the toolbox labeled for you. You're welcome to help each other brainstorm. Once you're both done, you can move on to the remainder of the exercises in this chapter.

Often, the things we do to soothe ourselves are so automatic that we don't realize that we're coping, so I've provided these prompts to help you identify your coping skills.

What are some things that immediately put a smile on your face?

When you were a child, how did your caregivers console you?

What do you want your partner to do for you when you're upset?

As a child, what did you usually do to make yourself feel better?

How do you typically relax?

Partner A's Coping Toolbox

Partner B's Coping Toolbox

After you're done, bookmark your toolbox so that you can easily refer back to it. As you progress through this workbook, you'll be returning to it for various purposes. You may continue to edit your list by adding to it as you discover more tools and crossing out ones that no longer serve you, or you may want to reference it when you're having difficulty managing in-the-moment emotions.

The better you are at restoring your PNS, the more secure you'll feel. Think back to the beginning of this chapter when I mentioned that security is the result of a *process* in which evidence of safety is so consistent that it becomes predictable. In other words, you trust that things will work out for you no matter what happens.

Though having confidence to restore your own sense of safety can bring you a good deal of security, it isn't adequate to fill the human need for supportive relationships. As self-sufficient as some people may like to boast about being, the truth is, we humans cannot make it on our own, especially when we're forced to face unpredictable events that bring us pain. This is why having relationship security is such an important part of achieving emotional security.

If while growing up, you frequently felt insecure about your caregiver's commitment to you, then you would often be stressed and looking for ways to gain their approval. Only when you got the affection you craved could you feel safe again, so the idea that "love is fragile and needs to be earned" would become the dominant theme in your approach toward relationships. This kind of a narrative about relationships will keep a person constantly looking for evidence of love, and never feeling satisfied because they don't know what security in a relationship looks or feels like.

Relationship security requires a personal willingness to trust your partnership. I'm not simply referring to your partner's faithfulness, though fidelity is one type of security, but rather to trust in the capacity and resilience of your partnership to weather any storm. This type of security can only be achieved over a long period of facing and overcoming challenges together. This is precisely why you and your partner need to learn to collaboratively work through differences by removing the emotional obstacles brought on by your fight-or-flight response. With each successful resolution of a problem, you grow more confident in the strength of your partnership, and your sense of security grows stronger.

Chances are, there are areas of your relationship where security exists, but you just haven't learned to find value in them yet. This following exercise will ask you a series of questions to help you connect with areas of your relationship where you may already have some security.

You will both work on this exercise at the same time and will need something separate to write on. I recommend that you read and respond to each question privately. Once you've both completed your parts, you may come together to share your answers before moving on.

Briefly write about a poor relationship you've had in the past. This can be a past romantic partner, friends, coworker, or family member.

What felt bad to you about the relationship?

Do you have those same struggles in your current relationship with your partner?

If not, what does your partner provide in your relationship so that you don't need to feel that way?

If so, what do you need from your partner to not have to feel that way?

What worries did you have in past relationships that you don't have to worry about in your current one?

What do your responses say about the areas of your relationship you feel secure in?

The main objective of these two chapters was to help you develop an understanding of and confidence over the internal processes of your nervous system that drive your behaviors. The more awareness you have of your internal world, the better control you'll have over how you engage with others, and the more success you'll have in nurturing the safe platform you and your partner need to connect intimately. As you work through this book, you'll both continue to develop your confidence to deal with upsetting emotions, so you're well on your way toward achieving emotional security. But remember that true emotional security requires both self-trust and at least one supportive relationship to be achieved. In part 2 of this book, you and your partner will begin to develop relational skills that will help satisfy each other's need to feel secure in a relationship.

Thus far in this workbook, I've talked a lot what can happen to an adult who suffered unmet emotional needs during childhood. Because a child's understanding of the world is so limited, they need concrete evidence that they are loved unconditionally in order to feel secure, and they gain that evidence through fulfillment of these five emotional needs by their primary caregivers:

- Emotional attunement
- Acknowledgment
- Unconditional acceptance
- Responsiveness
- Warmth

Our childhood caregiver's ability to meet these five emotional needs for us set the tone for the way we'd later show up in relationships throughout life, and impacts our perceptions about what we should expect and how we should treat others in intimate relationships. So if your caregiver had healthy relational skills, you were not only familiar with the feeling of safety but also adopted tools to nurture safe and pleasant conditions for those around you. Because humans naturally gravitate toward things that make them feel comfortable, developing healthy RQ tools will help support a warm base that the two of you will be naturally drawn to, without conscious effort.

The more successful a caregiver was at meeting those five needs for us, the more comfortable we are in our own skin, and the more tools we have to navigate relationship ups and downs.

However, when our emotional needs were not adequately met during childhood, an unexplainable and inconsolable emptiness exists in place of those unmet needs, and throughout our lives, we are left without meaningful tools to fill the void within ourselves and our relationships.

To rectify this, the solution is not to find a *perfect* partner to satisfy all of your desires, but to have corrective relationship experiences with a partner who's just as invested in developing a secure relationship with you as you are with them. In part 2 of this book, you'll learn all the tools that the two of you need to foster the safe and secure relationship that you've both deserved all along. Through practice exercises, you'll begin to develop the tools that will allow you to both experience and meet these five emotional needs for each other, in the same way you would have done if these needs had been met for you during childhood.

Time for a Pause

Before you continue on to part 2, let's pause and reflect on the material and self-knowledge you've acquired over the past several weeks. If either of you feel unsure about any of the chapters or concepts, you should go back to review before continuing on. Repeat the entire chapter if that feels appropriate. If you both feel ready to move on, I encourage you to continue practicing appreciation of each other, and keep working on building awareness of your own and your partner's emotional states. While the exercises in this book encourage practice, mastery only comes from putting knowledge into action.

Here are some things to work on until your next workbook session:

- Bring awareness to the times you feel good around your partner, and use words to describe the experience. How do you feel? What do you like about it?
- Pay attention to times when you experience unpleasant feelings and what you do when you feel those feelings.
- What are healthy things you do to cope with uncomfortable feelings? How about unhealthy things?
- What's something new you've learned thus far, no matter how minor? How can it be applied to improve your relationship?

Checking In

Welcome back! In the last workbook session, you were asked to continue practice by paying attention to your internal physical and emotional processes. You guided each other through relaxation exercises to build awareness of how your mind and body respond to stress, and are thus taking positive steps to manage your relationship interactions with more purpose.

Engage each other in a guided discussion about your progress by taking turns responding to the questions below. Be thoughtful about your responses, but don't spend too much time on them.

On a scale of 1 (dissatisfied) to 5 (very satisfied), how do you rate your relationship interactions since the last time you worked in this book?

As a team, what did you do well together this week?

In what ways has working on this book affected your relationship thus far?

What's something you can do better for your relationship this week?

Share one thing that made you appreciate your partner this week.

The Five Emotional Needs

Most of the content covered in part 1 focused on developing a deep understanding of emotional security and bridging how your relevant life experiences could impact the way you engage in intimate relationships today. To feel truly secure in your adult relationships, your caregivers would have had to meet specific needs for you during childhood. Here in part 2, you'll learn what those needs are and begin to develop the kind of relationship IQ (RQ) that a person raised by emotionally intelligent caregivers would have acquired.

Though a perfect caregiver doesn't exist, the more intuitive your caregiver was about your needs, the more tools you had to navigate relationships with. In fact, it's very likely that you already possess relationship skills that have worked well for you, in which case the chapters in this section might serve to validate or enhance what you already know and practice in your present relationship.

However, no amount of emotional competence from your caregivers could be enough to fully prepare you for the unpredictable world you'd eventually need to face. The best that your caregiver could have done was set you up for success by providing a safe environment and life skills to deal with adversity and nurture fulfilling relationships, but you would *still* need to improvise. This means we *all* need to learn to navigate uncertainties, and though some are better equipped from the start, others are simply further back on the continuum of RQ skills, and can still develop the tools necessary to achieve true relationship security. This is where you start.

CHAPTER 4

Emotional Attunement

Emotional attunement is an individual's ability to sense another's emotional state and adequately tend to their needs. A caregiver who is emotionally attuned can read their child's emotional cues and respond appropriately to their needs. If their child is happy, the caregiver will join in their joy; if their child is troubled, they will make efforts to alleviate their distress.

As young children, we needed our caregivers to attune to our emotions because of how limited we were in communication. Especially in early infancy, our comfort level was at the complete mercy of our caregivers. The better they could decipher our needs, the more comfortable and safe we felt.

To be clear, emotionally attuned caregivers are not telepathic; rather, they're skillful at dealing with emotions, whether their own or others. Unlike the less emotionally competent caregivers who become overwhelmed at the sound of their child's cries, attuned caregivers are confident about their ability to calm their child because they have taken the time to learn their child's cues. They might listen to subtle shifts in the tone of their cries or make note of things their child responds well to. Over time these caregivers become more intuitive about how to comfort their child, which reassures the child that unpleasant feelings are manageable and will eventually go away.

One of the many things an attuned caregiver does to reassure their child's safety in a big and unfamiliar world is to provide guidance by dialoguing with them. Though reciprocal verbal communication may not be possible, attuned caregivers still speak to their children to demonstrate their presence, and to help them make sense of their emotional experiences and develop language.

Over time, children of attuned caregivers view language as a primary means to get their needs met, and through ongoing practice, are able to better articulate their needs due to an expanding vocabulary. In adult relationships, good communication skills promote meaningful discussions that lead to healthy communication of needs, increased chances of having needs met, and deeper knowing of each other. The result of this level of understanding of a person is what we call intimacy.

Children who aren't provided words to convey how they feel are less confident about the likelihood of having their needs met; they not only struggle to communicate effectively but also frequently don't even understand why they feel the way they do. As a result, they may become easily stressed and miscommunicate, shut down, or attempt to act out uncomfortable feelings through aggression.

In the same way that an emotionally attuned caregiver develops intuitions about their child by reading their emotional cues, you and your partner can develop more intimacy by getting to know each other more on an emotional level.

To do so, the most basic thing you can do is to begin incorporating more feelings vocabulary in your daily conversations. Though you may not always be consciously aware of them, there are emotions attached to every experience you have. The more you talk about your emotional experiences, the better your partner understands your internal world, and the more effortless it eventually becomes to meet each other's needs.

Here's a list of feelings that are common to our everyday lives. Take a moment to read them out loud with your partner. Some words might bring up stronger feelings than others, so pay attention to what might be going on internally. Below the list of feelings is a short discussion for practice.

Accused
Angry
Annoyed
Anxious
Apathetic
Ashamed
Bored
Close
Confident
Connected
Desperate
Disappointed
Disconnected
Disgusted
Elated
Excited
Exhausted
Fortunate
Frustrated
Grateful
Guilty
Helpless
Hopeless
Hostile
Indifferent
Invisible
Irritated
Jealous
Joyful
Left out
Lonely
Misunderstood
Nervous
Numb
Overwhelmed
Powerless
Rejected
Resentful
Sad
Surprised
Suspicious
Tired
Unappreciated
Unheard
Unmotivated
Used
Unimportant
Worried

If either of you can think of feelings you commonly experience that are not on this list, write them down here:

____

____

____

Decide which of you will go first, and swap roles when done.

Supporting partner, read the questions to your partner and assist by writing down their responses where space is provided.

Select three feelings that brought up the strongest internal response.

Partner A: ______________________________

____

Partner B: ______________________________

____

Select one of those three feelings, and share about an incident where you felt that way.

(Instead of writing down your partner's story verbatim, use your own words to repeat back what your partner shared. Check with your partner if you got the story correct.)

This brief exercise was designed to give you an idea of what it might feel like to use feelings words to share a story. Feelings words give the listener a deeper level of understanding of your experiences. If you weren't encouraged to talk about your feelings while growing up, you might not know what it's like to deeply connect with somebody, and you might instead get caught up sharing details that give very little information about who you are and how you perceive things. To help others get to know you on a more intimate level and add more meaning to your conversations, try to expand on how you *felt* about an incident, or provide some context on *why* you're sharing a particular story.

While developing proper language to convey your feelings more accurately can help improve overall comprehension of each other's needs, you can further deepen understanding by learning to listen with intent.

Attuned caregivers are invested in getting to know their children deeply and do so by making continuous efforts to understand them throughout their development. During infancy, that might look like reading their facial expressions and paying attention to their signs of distress, and as their children get older, they *listen*. Attuned caregivers don't just hear the words spoken by their children, they *actively* listen. They're dedicated to figuring out what their children are trying to tell them with their limited vocabulary, and do so by giving them their undivided attention, asking questions to clarify what they understand, and giving them time to think about what they're trying to say.

Children whose caregivers use active listening to engage with them feel important, understood, and safe to openly share their thoughts and feelings. When upset, they're accustomed to using their words to resolve their discomforts. These children grow to become adults who think before they speak or act, and are good at communicating and listening.

You may not have noticed, but you've already begun to develop your active listening skills simply by following instructions in these workbook exercises. Whenever you were asked to paraphrase what your partner was saying, you were listening intently and trying to find meaning behind your partner's messages. This skill is something that you'll continue to practice throughout the remainder of this workbook, and hopefully in your relationship interactions.

And though there are many other important active listening skills, there's one that's especially important to building intimacy: *empathy*. Empathy is the ability to imagine what another person is thinking or feeling, and it is crucial to the formation of safe and supportive relationships. Caregivers who empathize with their children are able to momentarily suspend their own perspectives so they can try to see things through their children's lens. This allows them to more accurately understand the nuances of their children's struggles and find appropriate solutions to resolve their discomforts. Caregiver empathy is important to children's security; remember that very young children are incapable of advocating for themselves, so the more empathic their caregivers are, the better they can meet their children's needs.

Like an empathic caregiver who would momentarily suspend their own perspectives to understand the needs of their child, you too can learn to temporarily set aside your own views in order to see where your partner could be coming from. The following exercise will help you with that.

In this exercise, though you'll still be designated a *supporting* or *practicing* role, you'll both have an active part. Decide who will take which role first, and swap roles when completed.

Supporting partner, guide your partner through this exercise by reading the prompts out loud, and respond to questions for yourself when prompted to.

> *This exercise is designed to help the two of us empathize with each other. I'll be asking you to share things that might bring up some discomfort. As you share your story, try and notice any internal sensations that might be present. You may choose to stop at any time.*
>
> *Share an upsetting memory from your childhood. Try to take me back to the experience, and help me understand what the experience was like for you.*
>
> *(Give your partner some time to think and share their story.)*

What was coming up internally as you were telling the story? Physical sensations? Thoughts?

(Paraphrase your partner's story, and ask for clarification from your partner if necessary. Try to relate to your partner's story by suspending your own perspective for a moment and imagining yourself in their shoes. Share with your partner what you understand about why they felt the way they did.)

Especially if you or your partner are not yet skilled at talking about your feelings, it could be helpful to ask questions to deepen understanding. To truly empathize with another person, you want to have a good idea of what they think and how they feel about things. Empathic caregivers are dedicated to knowing their children intimately, and are curious about their inner world, so their questions aim to understand *how* versus *what* their children experience. You can ask questions like these to deepen understanding of your partner's experiences:

What was that like for you?

What was going through your mind in that moment?

What do you think about that?

How did that make you feel?

What does that mean to you?

Why do you think that's so important for you?

What do you mean by that?

How do you feel about it now?

How did you get through that?

Empathic caregivers also validate their children's feelings by verbally acknowledging that their needs are reasonable. Whenever caregivers validate their children's feelings, it legitimizes what they feel internally and gives them certainty that their feelings are real and therefore deserve to be tended to. Validating statements sound like these:

- "It makes sense that you'd feel that way."
- "I can see why you'd think that."

- "That's a reasonable way to look at it."
- "I would feel that way too if I were in your position."
- "It's normal to feel scared in a situation like that."
- "I don't blame you at all for believing that."
- "If I were in your shoes, I would feel..."

Children whose needs are consistently met and validated grow to become adults who trust their own perspectives and aren't afraid to speak up in the presence of disagreements, increasing the chances that their needs are both heard and addressed. Children raised by less empathic caregivers, on the other hand, are less confident about their own perspectives and therefore less likely to ask for what they want because they are not sure if their needs are valid. These caregivers would mostly engage with their child through their own adult lens, and tend to assume that their child's wants and feelings were negligible. For example, they might call their young child "silly" for being afraid to start school because they could not recognize how scary it could be for young children to be left alone in unfamiliar environments. Nonempathic caregivers are not "bad" caregivers; they just don't know how to ease their child's distress, and their solutions are often aimed at trying to shut down the child's emotions, which makes the child feel as if their feelings are wrong or unwanted. Here are some examples of things a nonempathic caregiver might say in response to their child's emotional distress:

- "You're silly, you have nothing to be afraid of."
- "That's no reason to cry."
- "You're just too sensitive."
- "Stop crying!"
- "You shouldn't be upset about that."

Remember from chapter 2 that emotions are a person's *subjective* response to certain stimuli, meaning that people respond to things based on their unique personal experiences. Therefore, your emotions are *always* valid, even if others don't have the same emotional response as you.

When children are taught to question or restrain their emotions, they miss out on opportunities to develop healthy tools to resolve their discomforts. When they reach adulthood, the mere presence of uncomfortable emotions would be stressful because they don't have any confidence in their ability to manage how they feel.

To truly resolve your unmet needs, you must first accept that your feelings are valid so that you can begin to find appropriate solutions to address them. The following discussion will help you and your partner begin to trust your feelings and learn to validate each other's experiences.

Decide what role you'll each play first, and swap roles when you're done.

Supporting partner, read the following prompts aloud, and use one of the validating statements you read earlier to validate your partner's feelings. If you can come up with your own validating statement, please feel free to use it. For this exercise, there is no need to write down responses, but you will be asked to respond to some questions.

> *Talk about somebody who brings up uncomfortable feelings in you. What do you think about them? What don't you like about them? Share a brief story to illustrate your point.*
>
> *(Paraphrase what your partner just shared with you by highlighting what you think are the most important points of your partner's story. Using one of the validating statements listed above, provide your partner with some validation for the way they feel.)*

Every time you validate your partner's feelings, you provide more reassurance to each other that it's safe to openly share feelings, which makes you both feel as though your needs are heard and taken seriously and makes it possible to address and tackle problems that can otherwise harm the relationship.

In this chapter, you learned about emotional attunement, which is the first of five important emotional needs that all children must have fulfilled in order to feel safe and secure with their caregivers. Caregivers who are emotionally attuned to their children are invested in knowing their children deeply, and use skills such as communication, curiosity, and empathy to do so. Over time, these caregivers develop intuitions that help them meet their children's needs with more ease. On the receiving end, children raised by attuned caregivers feel safe and secure because they feel seen by them, and therefore trust that their needs will be met. As a result, these children tend to grow up to be emotionally competent adults who are knowledgeable about their own feelings, can articulate their needs well, and also know how to be safe sources of support for others.

Time for a Pause

We'll take a break here to let some of this material settle. For continuing practice, engage in more meaningful discussion with each other using the skills you learned. Set aside time to initiate conversations. Here are suggested practices to integrate emotional attunement into your relationship this week:

- Each time you share or listen to a story, consider the emotional experiences by either using feelings words, or asking your partner to use feelings words.
- When listening to your partner share, connect more deeply with their story by imagining yourself in their position, and practice more validating statements.
- Look for signs that your partner already attunes to your feelings.

Checking In

Over your break, you were encouraged to continue practicing some of the tools that a person would've picked up from being raised by an emotionally attuned caregiver. Specifically, you were asked to try to engage in more meaningful discussions by using feelings words, asking deepening questions, and validating your partner's experiences.

Engage each other in a discussion about progress by taking turns responding to the questions below. Be thoughtful about your responses, but don't spend too much time on them.

On a scale of 1 (dissatisfied) to 5 (very satisfied), how do you rate your relationship interactions since the last time you worked in this book?

In what ways did you try to incorporate emotional attunement in your relationship? How did it go?

In what ways did you notice your partner trying to incorporate emotional attunement? How did they do?

Looking back at this week, what's a situation that you or your partner could have practiced attunement?

What will you do to continue working on developing emotional attunement?

Share one thing your partner did this week that you appreciated.

CHAPTER 5

Acknowledgment

Acknowledgment refers to the act of honoring another's inherent worth. Caregivers who acknowledge their children recognize them as individuals who are entitled to their own feelings, opinions, and perspectives. These caregivers tend to promote egalitarian home environments where everybody's needs are considered. They understand the importance of individual identity development, so when appropriate, they encourage self-expression by giving their children choices and space to speak up about their likes and dislikes.

Children raised in households like these are confident about what they want and feel justified speaking up for it. In adulthood, this would translate to good boundaries and assertive communication of needs.

Caregivers who are less emotionally attuned to the needs of their children tend to foster home environments that are hierarchical, where certain family members have more decision-making power than others. In family systems like this, the primary caregiver often feels responsible, and perhaps entitled, to make decisions on behalf of their children, not realizing the damage that their efforts have on their children's emotional development.

To feel safe and secure, children need to have some agency over their lives so they know that the things they do and say have some impact on their environment. For example, if a child asks their caregiver to stop tickling them and their caregiver indeed stops, the child would feel as though their words have power. How worthy children feel depends heavily on the way their caregivers respect their autonomy and existence as they are growing up. Without freedom to make their own decisions, children feel disempowered and lack a sense of self; they don't have a clear idea of what they value, what they're good at, and what they need to feel comfortable.

Although in a healthy partnership, we should strive to consider our partners in all our decisions, we must also have some liberty to pursue things that are personally fulfilling and be able to protect ourselves from things we're uncomfortable with. We do this by knowing our personal limits and honoring our right to enforce those limits with healthy boundaries. In the following exercise, you will both begin to reflect upon and clarify your own personal values.

Decide which role you each will play, and swap roles after the set of questions are answered.

Supporting partner, read the prompts and assist your partner by writing down responses where space is provided. If no space is provided, simply listen.

In no particular order, list five things that are very important to you.

*Partner A:*______________________________

____

*Partner B:*______________________________

____

Think of a person from any point in your life who ever made you feel angry, and share a story illustrating how they made you feel that way.

What does that story tell you about what's unacceptable to you?

*Partner A:*______________________________

____

*Partner B:*______________________________

____

Think of a person from any point in your life who ever made you feel disgust, and share a story illustrating how they made you feel that way.

What does that story tell you about what makes you uncomfortable?

*Partner A:*____

____

*Partner B:*____

____

Think of a person from any point in your life who ever made you feel annoyed, and share a story illustrating how they made you feel that way.

What does that story tell you about what you don't like?

*Partner A:*____

____

*Partner B:*____

____

Information gathered from this exercise gives you both an idea of what's important to each other, and can be helpful to guide relationship decisions that affect both you and your partner. To continue exploring your boundaries, pay special attention to the kinds of situations that might trigger sensations associated with your stress response, and be curious about what those feelings are trying to tell you about where your boundaries are.

Whether you've been actively enforcing them or not, you have a set of personal limits that are unique to you and result from your values and experiences. What's acceptable to one person may not be acceptable to the next, so having open discussions with your partner about things you're okay and not okay with takes the guesswork out of how to have a good relationship with each other. If it feels like it takes conscious effort to identify situations that make you uncomfortable, there's a high chance that you grew up having your feelings and needs neglected.

If caregivers didn't acknowledge children's feelings about things, they were not likely to believe that their feelings mattered. Often, this means that decisions for the family were made by one person without any open discussion or concern about what others wanted. These children would later become adults who don't see collaboration as a means to overcome relationship challenges. When confronted with a problem, they might feel soley responsible to find solutions for everybody, or avoid contributing overall. Habits like these tend to give way to power imbalance in relationships, and can lead to a slew of problems, including resentment and overall dissatisfaction.

Acknowledging caregivers demonstrate to their children that they matter by treating them as special and individual beings. They're interested in knowing things about their children, such as how they think and what they're good at, and approach them with curiosity. Whenever there are decisions to be made for the family, or topics of common interest, these caregivers involve their children by explaining things in a way they'll understand, and asking for their input when appropriate. When children are included in family matters that way, they feel like they matter. This gives them a secure feeling of *belonging*—that there's a place for them in the family.

In the same way that an acknowledging caregiver involves their children in discussions, you can also foster a collaborative relationship with your partner by engaging in more open dialogue where both of your valuable perspectives are heard and factored into important decisions.

This list suggests open-ended questions or things to say to be more welcoming of your partner's input. Review the list with each other out loud, and see if any of the suggestions can be useful in the next exercise to expand your understanding of your partner's perspectives.

"I'm not sure about ____________________. How do you feel?"

"What's your opinion on ____________________?"

"Can you expand a bit more on that?"

"What do you think about ____________________?"

"What ideas do you have about how we should handle ____________________?"

"What problems do you see with that?"

"What do you think?"

"What are our options?"

This exercise will ask you and your partner to talk about important topics that can sometimes stir up conflict when left unexamined. For the first part of the exercise, you'll individually answer the following questions using a separate journal or sheet of paper. When you're both done, you may move on to the next part of the exercise.

How do you think money should be handled in a romantic partnership? Why does this make sense to you?

What are your feelings about your partner maintaining friendships with exes? What's the reasoning behind your perspective?

What kind of lifestyle do you want to see for the two of you in ten years? Why does this appeal to you?

What is something you admire about your partner? What does this mean in terms of what strength(s) they have?

Once you've each answered these questions on your own, engage each other in a discussion by taking turns reading and answering the questions that follow. Keep in mind that only one person should be answering at once, which means that when one partner is speaking, the other should be *actively* listening without interruption. If you need help understanding your partner's perspective, refer to the list of suggestions above to invite your partner to expand more on what they have to say. Respond to the questions according to your chosen identifier.

Partner A, how do you think money should generally be handled in a romantic partnership? Why does this make sense to you?

Partner B, what value can you take away from your partner's perspective?

Partner B, how do you think money should generally be handled in a romantic partnership? Why does this make sense to you?

Partner B, what are your feelings about your partner maintaining friendships with exes? What's the reasoning behind your perspective?

Partner A, what value can you take away from your partner's perspective?

Partner A, what are your feelings about your partner maintaining friendships with exes? What's the reasoning behind your perspectives?

Partner A, what kind of lifestyle do you want to see for the two of you in ten years? Why does this appeal to you?

Partner B, what value can you take away from your partner's vision?

Partner B, what kind of lifestyle do you want to see for the two of you in ten years? Why does this appeal to you?

Partner B, what is something that you admire about your partner? What does this mean in terms of what strength(s) they have?

Partner A, what do you have to say about what your partner just said about you?

Partner A, what is something that you admire about your partner? What does this mean in terms of what strength(s) they have?

Partner B, what do you have to say about what your partner just said about you?

This exercise was designed to initiate a preliminary discussion about topics that are typically uncomfortable yet important to address. As relationships mature and security grows, feelings about various topics evolve with it, so it's healthy to continually practice having open discussions about sensitive issues. The more you talk about these things, the better you'll both get at having difficult conversations. If you need ideas on boundaries to discuss, here are some common relationship questions that every couple should address at some point, along with some relevant examples:

- What are things that should remain private (sharing passwords, cellphone access)?
- What is considered inappropriate social media behavior (posting photos, liking/commenting, meeting new people)?
- What is considered cheating (flirting, hugging, image texting)?
- When is it okay to go out without each other (happy hour, traveling)?
- What are your boundaries surrounding physical touch (public displays of affection, sex)?
- What are our values about parenting (grandparent involvement, religion, spanking)?

Finally, and most importantly, acknowledging caregivers honor their children as individual beings by holding themselves accountable. These caregivers recognize that although children lack understanding of how the world works, their emotions matter and deserve to be taken care of. They show accountability by practicing restraint in the treatment of their children, and by accepting responsibility when they've hurt them.

Because children are so defenseless, they need to trust that their caregivers are concerned about their feelings and will not use their dominance to overpower them. Children whose caregivers fail to acknowledge their feelings are unlikely to understand the value of emotional repair, and become adults who struggle to get past relationship setbacks, whether they were hurt or the one that caused the pain.

No matter how big or small an error, intentional or not, we must learn to acknowledge our partner's feelings. If we don't, they're left to question how vulnerable they are to being hurt again. To regain their trust, we must assure them that they're unlikely to be hurt the same way again, which can be done by taking accountability for the actions that led to hurting them.

While the word "sorry" can be a good start, an emotionally reparative apology must include these four steps:

- Acknowledgment of wrongdoing
- Clarifying intentions
- Showing understanding of the consequences of your actions
- Offering a plan for change

This is what it sounds like put together:

"I'm sorry that I ignored you. I was so tired when I came home that I just wanted to nap, and I realize that I made you feel invisible. Next time I'm tired, I'll let you know how much time I need to wind down."

Now it's your turn to try. Think about a time that you may have hurt or upset your partner. Using the four-step apology to acknowledge your partner's feelings, let them know how you plan to change. Either one of you can go first, and swap when you're done.

Supporting partner, read the prompts out loud and jot down your partner's response in your own words.

Recall a time when you hurt or upset me.

Partner A:____

____

Partner B:____

____

Explain what your original intentions were.

Partner A:____

____

Partner B:____

____

Acknowledge the consequences of your actions.

Partner A:____

____

Partner B:____

____

What do you plan to do to avoid upsetting me like that again?

*Partner A:*____

____

*Partner B:*____

____

Now that the both of you have completed your set of questions, try to integrate all of your responses into one apology statement, similar to the example I provided above. Take turns writing it down in the space provided, and read it out to your partner.

*Partner A:*____

____

____

____

____

*Partner B:*____

____

____

____

____

Being on the receiving end of such an apology helps restore safety because it demonstrates that our feelings matter and have an impact on our partner's future choices. This gives us confidence that they'll continue to take care of our feelings, which gives us the reassurance we need to continue being vulnerable. In the next chapter, you'll learn more about why vulnerability is so important to a secure and fulfilling relationship, and what it takes to get there.

Time for a Pause

Let's pause and put some of the things you learned into practice for the upcoming week. Over the break, you should continue staying mindful of your interactions with your partner. Pay attention to the things you appreciate about them, and let them know how their efforts make you feel. When you converse, invite each other into your inner worlds by using feelings words. Though it may sound like a lot, try not to stress about applying these skills all the time or perfectly. All you need to do is be more aware of situations where relationship IQ (RQ) skills could be useful, whether you try to implement them or not. Most importantly for this week, you should be working on a more collaborative relationship by doing the following:

- Look for ways to make collaborative decisions this week. For example, if you're always the one to choose dinner, what about asking your partner what they want?
- Pay attention to how you receive and respond to your partner when they talk about things you're not familiar with. Are you honoring their perspectives as worthy even though they don't align with yours?
- Look for signs that your partner makes you feel important or valued, and really take in those feelings as signs of safety.
- Notice times when you might feel uncomfortable or irritated. What do those feelings tell you about the kind of boundary you should set?

Checking In

Since the last workbook session, you worked on paying attention to your own emotional cues to identify different areas of your life where you might need to set some limits to feel safe. Boundaries are extremely important to your development of emotional security because they help *you* protect yourself from uncomfortable situations, and teach *your partner* how not to cause you discomfort.

Engage each other in a discussion about your progress as a couple by taking turns responding to the following questions. Be thoughtful about your responses, but also don't spend too much time on them.

On a scale of 1 (dissatisfied) to 5 (very satisfied), how do you rate your relationship interactions since the last time you worked in this book?

As a team, what did you do well together this week? What can you add to your Relationship Toolbox?

How did you attempt to value your partner's perspectives more this week?

In what ways did you notice your partner making more collaborative efforts this week?

Thinking back, were there situations where you could have made more room for either your own or your partner's perspectives?

What's one boundary you learned that you have?

What's one boundary you learned that your partner has?

Share one thing your partner did this week that you appreciated.

CHAPTER 6

Unconditional Acceptance

Unconditional acceptance is one person's commitment to loving another as they are and without any agenda. Caregivers who unconditionally accept their children always see them in the best light. They try to understand their children rather than punish their struggles. These caregivers give their children room to explore and grow through trial and error. When their children make mistakes, they try to understand their internal drives through compassion or curiosity. When their children misbehave, these caregivers provide patient instruction to correct their behavior.

Like all human beings, children are imperfect and evolving, and they need to have total faith that they're still loved no matter how much they stumble. On the receiving end of this type of caregiving, children feel safe to be their most honest, uninhibited selves because they trust their caregivers to understand their intentions and give them opportunities to take corrective measures. Because of their caregiver's steadfast loyalty, these children have the courage to put themselves in the kinds of vulnerable positions that promote personal and relational development.

Children who feel unconditionally accepted are likely to carry those feelings into adulthood in the form of self-acceptance. In adult relationships, this leads to stronger relationship intimacy because of the courage they have to share deeply private thoughts and feelings.

A major factor that can interfere with children's ability to be their carefree, vulnerable selves is how their caregivers respond to their imperfections. Although most caregivers are instinctually driven to protect their children, it's not always apparent in the way they treat them. Emotionally immature caregivers who struggle to manage the stress of their role tend to react negatively toward their children's perceived inadequacies.

From the perspective of a child who knows so little about the world, our caregiver's opinions about us carry immense weight, and therefore heavily influence how we see ourselves. Those who received a lot of negative feedback from their caregivers would've received the message that they're inherently flawed, and need to hide certain parts of themselves. They may have been criticized, teased, or shamed for a range of things, from the way they look to mistakes they made, and end up with insecurities of being *too much* of something or *not enough* of something else. If carried into adulthood, those hidden parts are viewed as threats to their relationships and sometimes even societal acceptance.

True relationship security requires that you feel confident about your partner's commitment to you under any condition. To develop this confidence, you must be willing to confront your insecurities and begin to show up as your whole self, including the parts that were deemed unacceptable by your caregivers. Only when you bring all parts of you to light will you be able to re-evaluate lifelong narratives about your insecurities that have been keeping you from feeling secure.

The following exercise will walk you through a series of questions to help you identify some of the personal traits you've believed you had to hide to avoid social rejection.

Here you have the option to work together aloud or if you don't feel comfortable, you may write your responses in your personal journal. You will still decide who will play which role first, and switch when you've completed the responses.

Supporting partner, read the prompts out loud to your partner, but give them the option to answer privately if they wish, in which case you can skip writing their responses in the spaces provided.

Can you recall memories of situations where you had to hold back or hide certain parts of you? What did you have to hold back or hide?

Partner A: ______________________________

____

Partner B: ______________________________

____

What do you believe having those insecurities mean about you as a person?

Partner A:____

____

Partner B:____

____

How does having those insecurities affect the way you engage in your relationships?

Partner A:____

____

Partner B:____

____

How do you attempt to hide those insecurities?

Partner A:____

____

Partner B:____

____

What are you afraid your partner would think if they saw that part of you?

*Partner A:*____

____

*Partner B:*____

____

How would things be different for you if, rather than hiding those traits, you accepted them as a part of you?

*Partner A:*____

____

*Partner B:*____

____

The truth is, human behavior is complex, and if you're worried that you're *too much* or *not enough* of something, it's probably a sign that you overcompensate somewhere on the extreme opposite end of the scale. For example, if you worry that you complain *too much*, then you'll probably try hard *never* to complain, and feel very self-conscious in the rare times you do express a grievance. That self-consciousness is the precursor to vulnerability, and it shows up whenever you're about to do something that you know could lead to you getting hurt or rejected.

To be vulnerable means taking an emotional risk. Like any risk worth taking, you expose yourself to the possibility of failing or getting hurt, but you also open up the path toward achieving what you really want.

As scary as it can feel, emotional vulnerability is the gateway to relationship security. Remember that part of feeling secure is knowing that we have access to support no matter what condition we're in. Only when the people we rely on for support see and accept us in our most vulnerable, uncensored state can we feel truly secure.

That's a lot easier said than done. Most of the time, our insecurities are deep seated, and over time, the walls we put up to protect those insecurities from being seen become stronger. Rather than ripping off the Band-Aid and expecting yourself to expose your secrets all at once, there's a clever way trick you can use to begin slowly building comfort. It's called the Share-Check-Share technique.* The goal is to take small, intentional risks to help build tolerance for dealing with vulnerability.

The premise is simple: When there's something you want to share or discuss with your partner but are concerned about their response, you can start by *sharing* a small part, then *checking* their response, and if comfortable, you can *share* a bit more. You can keep repeating this process until you gain the courage to complete what you want to say. This is what it might sound like:

Person 1: There's this movie idea I've always wanted to pitch.

Person 2: Oh yeah? What is it?

Person 1: Well, I feel weird talking about it.

Person 2: Why do you feel weird?

Person 1: Because I've never said it out loud before.

Person 2: Just tell me.

If you were in the position of Person 1, would you feel comfortable continuing? Some might, some might not. We all have our own levels of comfort, so when using this technique, listen to your inner instincts and let them guide you.

For example, let's say that Person 1 still didn't feel safe to continue and needed more reassurances before sharing more. In that case, they have the option to end the conversation there or communicate what they felt or needed in the moment.

Person 1: I'm worried that you're going to think it's dumb.

Here, rather than ending the conversation, Person 1 addressed their in-the-moment feeling. Speaking candidly about how you're feeling in a particular moment is a good strategy to address whatever emotional obstacle is present. Vulnerably sharing your in-the-moment feelings prompts your partner to be more sensitive in their approach.

---

* Whitfield, C. 1987. *Healing the Child Within: Discovery and Recovery for Adult Children of Dysfunctional Families*. Arlington, VA: Health Communications.

For this next exercise, you'll practice the Share-Check-Share technique by each selecting a topic from the list below to discuss with your partner. Review the list together before moving on. I challenge you to select a topic that at least makes you a little uncomfortable so you can actually experience what it feels like to work through your fears of being vulnerable.

- Share a sexual fantasy you have.
- Talk about one of your most embarrassing moments.
- What's something illegal you've done?
- Name a pet peeve of yours that your partner does.
- Talk about something you regret doing.
- What about the future do you fear most?
- What's something you've lied about?
- Talk about a time you knowingly hurt somebody.
- What's something you preach but have a hard time practicing?
- Name three things you want people to see in you.
- Name something you would change about yourself.
- What's a characteristic you dislike in others but see in yourself?
- What are you most worried that people will judge you for?
- What do you really think about yourself?
- Name something you've done in a past relationship that you're not proud of.
- What's one of the biggest lessons you've learned in life so far?
- Talk about a time you had a falling out with a friend. What happened?
- What's something you're having trouble letting go of?
- Talk about anything else you've been itching to share.

Once you've selected your topic, decide which of you will go first, and swap when you're done. After you've both completed the first set of questions, move on to the next set of questions for a joint discussion. As a reminder, don't forget to pay attention to your internal processes as you're sharing. If you're doing the exercise correctly, you should at least experience some internal shifts in your mind and body. Use whatever coping skills you need to get you through this exercise!

Supporting partner, your primary job is to actively listen by attuning to your partner's feelings and finding appropriate moments to give them reassurance and validation so they'll feel safe to continue sharing.

Practicing partner, this time, instead of your partner reading the questions out loud to you, you'll guide yourself by reading each prompt silently to yourself and then responding to it out loud. Also give your partner room to offer reassurance to you if that's what you need. The prompts are designed to sound much like the self-dialogue that would be going through your head when using the Share-Check-Share technique in practice.

Take a moment to think about the topic you've chosen and what relevant information you'd like your partner to know about you.

If you feel any resistance at all, label the feeling and let your partner know how you feel about sharing.

Tune in to your feelings. If you feel safe, start by sharing something small.

Look at your partner. How did they react?

Check back in with yourself. Do you feel safe to share more?

If you feel safe, go ahead and share a little more.

Check in on your partner again. What does their reaction tell you?

If you feel any resistance at all, let your partner know how you're feeling and what you need to continue.

If you feel safe to move on, share the next part of your story.

Repeat this process until you've completed what you wanted to share.

Once you've both shared your vulnerable topics with each other, you may continue with the following joint discussion. Decide who will play the supporting role first and swap roles when you're done.

How did it feel to share what you shared with me?

Have you ever thought about sharing that with me? Why or why not?

How did you think I would react?

Is there anything I did to support you that made it easier to keep sharing?

Is there anything I did that made it more difficult to keep sharing?

What are some takeaways from this exercise?

I hope that this exercise encouraged you to take more risks to be vulnerable with each other. I want to caution you that if you and your partner are not used to having vulnerable conversations with each other, you're not likely to have them perfectly every time from here on out. Expect your partner to still sometimes respond in ways that might make you feel unsafe, but trust that they're still learning. With more practice, you'll both get better at supporting each other.

To continue fostering emotional safety in your relationship, one of the best tools to have is compassion. Caregivers who are compassionate insist on seeing their children in a positive light, and strive to understand the intentions behind their less desirable behaviors. Because children are innocent and know so little about the world, they will do many things that complicate their caregiver's lives, so they need their caregivers to look past their mistakes and see the good in them. Here are examples of how a compassionate caregiver might respond after their child has made a mistake:

- "Oh no, sweetie, let me help you with that. Next time you have to ask for help, okay?"
- "Oh my gosh! Are you okay?"
- "I know you like to draw, but you can't draw on the walls. Here's some paper."
- "I think you did that because you were upset that they didn't want to play with you. What else could you have done?"

Responses like these make children feel safe because they show that their caregivers are understanding of their mistakes, and that they won't be abandoned as they *continue* to make mistakes.

Just like children need to know that they won't be abandoned for making mistakes, we adults need to know that our partners won't just leave us for our missteps or imperfections. You can learn to show your partner the same kind of understanding that a compassionate caregiver shows their children by asking yourself the following question each time you experience a negative feeling about them:

"If I assume that they were doing their best, what could I understand about this situation?"

Let's give it a try in this brief exercise. Either of you can go first, and swap when done.

Share a trait of mine that bothers you.

What assumptions have you made about me because of this trait?

If you were to assume that I'm doing my best, how else could you explain the reason that I have this trait?

The compassion you show your partner makes them feel comfortable around you because they don't need to be vigilant about hiding parts of themselves.

Compassion also makes forgiveness possible because it allows you to accept that your partner is imperfect and that they will make occasional mistakes.

Many people struggle to forgive because it makes them feel vulnerable. They worry that, once they forgive, they're vulnerable to being hurt again. To protect themselves, they put up their guard and block any opportunity for their partner to make reparations. This is often experienced by the wrongdoer as punishment, and creates an obstacle in the way of the couple having a comfortable, secure relationship.

Caregivers who unconditionally accept their children use compassion to forgive their children's mistakes. When their children behave poorly, these caregivers make efforts to understand the reasons behind their behaviors, explain the consequences of their actions, and provide corrective measures to right their wrongs. These efforts reassure children that when they disappoint their caregivers the relationship hasn't been forever ruined, and there's a path to reconciliation.

Similarly in adult relationships, forgiveness is much more than a simple statement of forgiveness. It's a long-term action plan that results in both partners' ability to make sense of the offense, and recognize the detrimental effects of it. Trust can be rebuilt when it's apparent that your partner understands the impact of their actions, and sincerity is reflected in their actions.

I'd like to reiterate that this book is not designed to handle topics of a heavy or sensitive nature. If you and your partner need help working through a painful betrayal, you should seek professional help. However, in all forms of reparative efforts, good communication of feelings is key. The better you are at describing the impact their actions have on you, the more they'll understand why change is necessary to have a good relationship with you.

Here's an exercise that can help you begin to find words to express pain to your partner. Decide which of you will go first, and switch roles when completed.

Supporting partner, read the questions out loud to your partner. As your partner is talking, be present and listen actively. Listen not only to their words but also to the emotions and meaning behind their words. Imagine yourself in their shoes, and provide validation where appropriate. There's no need to write down any responses.

Tell me about a time when I hurt you. Try to think of an example that's not too emotionally heavy.

(*For your partner's next two responses, see if there's a place to validate their feelings.*)

How did I make you feel?

What did it mean to you that I did that?

How did it affect other aspects of your life? Did it change anything for you?

Have we fully recovered from that? If so, what did I do to get there? If not, what can I do to make things better?

Supporting partner, using empathic language, what do you understand about why your partner was hurt?

In this chapter, we discussed the importance of unconditional acceptance and the way it liberates a person to show up as their most comfortable, honest selves. You learned about vulnerability and what interferes with it, and you practiced being vulnerable with each other. You practiced how to be compassionate toward each other, and how to use it toward forgiveness. These are extremely powerful tools that will help the two of you overcome challenges together. By challenging yourself to be open and making mutual efforts to understand and work with each other's imperfections, you develop a level of intimacy that is unrivaled by any other relationship. The result of these ongoing efforts is that you'll begin to trust and lean on each other for issues that nobody else is quite as equipped to help with, ultimately contributing to the security you seek in your relationship.

Time for a Pause

Let's stop here and discuss a plan for practice the upcoming week. Keep paying attention to the things you appreciate about your partner. Focus on incorporating more feelings into your conversations with each other. Keep tuning into your internal processes and be curious about what they're trying to tell you about a situation. What do you feel in your body? What kinds of thoughts are you having? Particularly this week, continue practicing unconditional acceptance by doing the following:

- Pay attention to negative judgments you have about yourself or your partner, and be curious about where those messages might come from. What's a more compassionate way to view the situation?
- Notice times when you hold yourself back from speaking your mind, and think about what you expect your partner to do or say in response. How can you implement Share-Check-Share?
- Look for signs that your partner already accepts certain parts of you that you're insecure about, and immerse yourself in the feeling of safety.
- If an opportunity arises, engage your partner in more discussions from the list of vulnerable topics.

Checking In

You've now learned about unconditional acceptance, and how it relates to your level of vulnerability in future relationships. You also learned about ways that compassion and forgiveness can support a more vulnerable relationship. Over the week, your assignment was to challenge yourself to be more vulnerable with your partner by paying attention to times you hold back, and to practice more compassion toward yourself and your partner.

Engage each other in a discussion about your progress as a couple by taking turns responding to the questions below. Be thoughtful about your responses, but also don't spend too much time on them.

On a scale of 1 (dissatisfied) to 5 (very satisfied), how do you rate your relationship interactions since the last time you worked in this book?

As a team, what did you do well together this week? What can you add to your Relationship Toolbox?

In what ways did you practice being vulnerable? How did it go?

In what ways did you practice acceptance this week? How difficult was it?

Talk about a situation where you could have practiced more compassion or acceptance of yourself or your partner.

In what situations did you wish your partner could have practiced more acceptance of you?

What's something you can do better for your relationship this week?

Share one thing your partner did this week that you appreciated.

CHAPTER 7

Responsiveness

Responsiveness in a relationship involves acknowledging your partner's bid for attention and providing appropriate support. Responsive caregivers are attentive to their children's needs, and develop their independence by identifying times when they struggle and providing age-appropriate assistance. Though their primary objective is to guide their children toward self-sufficiency, these caregivers continue to be accessible no matter what stage in life their children are in because they understand that everybody needs a safe place to land when life gets overwhelming.

A caregiver's level of responsiveness is crucial to a child's feeling of security because children need a guarantee that somebody will have their back if something bad happens. Each time their caregivers respond to their calls for help, these children develop more tolerance for being independent because they trust that their caregivers are accessible when needed. The safety net provided by accessible caregivers makes children less afraid to take the kinds of risks that are necessary for personal development. As these children grow in self-sufficiency they need less from their caregivers, but they can also recognize appropriate circumstances when help is needed. By adulthood, they understand the value of supportive relationships, and are just as comfortable receiving help as they are giving it.

Raising a child who's comfortable with interdependency can be a difficult task for caregivers because there's no perfect formula to do so, and too much or too little support can result in a child expecting too much or too little out of relationships.

Unresponsive caregivers tend to have expectations that are too high, and they may even lean on their children for various forms of support when they struggle to balance their obligations. Perhaps they have demanding jobs or an incapacitating illness, or are not ready to take on the full responsibilities of caregiving. Because of this, they may use their children as confidants, expect them to care for themselves, or even place them in the role of a stand-in parent for their siblings.

Due to unrealistically high expectations, children of unresponsive caregivers tend to be resourceful and efficient, but they are also prone to chronic stress because they can never depend on others for help. They may find it easier to do things on their own, struggle to recognize situations where help is warranted, and highly value the idea of being responsible and independent. As adults, they struggle to ask for help and rarely turn to their partners for help of any kind.

On the other hand, caregivers who are *too* available tend to be overbearing and provide little room for their children to develop independence and identity. They might do everything for their children, and aim to remove obstacles rather than teach their children how to overcome them. Though usually with good intentions, these caregivers' attempts to protect their children from discomfort deprives them of the kinds of challenges that are necessary to become self-sufficient.

Due to the caregiver's level of involvement in their care, these children grow to become adults who believe that relationships are all about caring for others. Though they're able to comprehend the significance of supportive relationships, the disproportionate amount of energy they place on caring for others means that their capacity to care for themselves remains underdeveloped. When faced with difficulty, they immediately seek out the support of others and are overcome with anxiety when support is not available.

In both styles of caregiving, children fail to recognize proper use of support, which can have negative impacts on their relationships in adulthood. Those adults who tend to take on too many responsibilities are prone to burnout, and more importantly, they deprive their partners of opportunities to feel useful, causing them to question how valuable they are to the relationship. On the flip side, adults who struggle with independence may overburden their closest relationships by placing too many responsibilities on others to care for them.

Among the important differences between an adequately responsive caregiver and one who's not is in *how* they initially respond to their children's needs. Unresponsive caregivers may ignore or minimize their children's needs and overbearing caregivers may over-involve themselves, while adequately responsive caregivers are warm and welcoming. When their children want to connect, they give their full attention and reciprocate by showing genuine interest in what their children want to share. When their children are in distress, they respond with concern and make efforts to soothe their discomfort. This makes children feel safe to approach them when they encounter difficulties.

Children raised in such environments grow to become adults who feel adequately supported, and therefore have capacity to give support, which promotes healthy interdependency. Interdependent relationships bring the highest level of security; not only does the person receiving help benefit from that support, but the person giving help also feels valued.

Like a responsive caregiver, you can nurture a safe environment for interdependent reliance by learning to respond warmly and adequately to your partner's needs, even if their complaints are about *you*. This does not mean that you need to take full responsibility for solving their problems, or to neglect your own needs to tend to theirs, but rather, to respond with genuine concern and focus your attention on understanding *their* pain when they're seeking support.

Before we do that, let's take a brief moment to reflect on how responsive *your* caregivers were while you were growing up, and see how your upbringing could impact the ways you use support in your relationship. Decide who will go first, and swap roles when completed.

Supporting partner, read the questions aloud to your partner. If it feels appropriate, try to offer supportive feedback based on what you've learned so far about active listening.

When you think back to your childhood, what was your relationship with your caregiver(s) like?

How did they respond when you got hurt or sick?

Share about a time when you were upset about something. How did your caregiver(s) respond to it?

How did they usually respond when you tried to share things with them?

How comfortable did you feel asking your caregiver(s) for things/help?

How did you feel when you were separated from your caregiver(s)?

The questions you and your partner just responded to should give you an idea of how accessible your childhood caregivers were, and how that now affects the way you seek support from your partner. If you were raised by an adequately responsive caregiver, you're likely comfortable operating in an interdependent relationship, and have a healthy balance of giving and receiving support. But if you were raised to be either overly independent or overly reliant, you may struggle to respond appropriately to your partner's needs or grievances.

How a person responds to your needs can have a great impact on your willingness to ask them for help in the future. Below are examples of the kinds of responses that may discourage a person from seeking support from their partners:

- Responding defensively or taking it personally when complaints are about them
- Giving unsolicited advice/information/solutions
- Being judgmental or critical
- Lecturing
- Blaming
- Minimizing or being dismissive of the problem
- Being distracted and not giving full attention
- Being annoyed

To create a welcoming environment that promotes interdependency, you should be approachable, present, and open to supporting your partner in a way that feels helpful to them. The following exercise will help the two of you reflect on your level of approachability, and teach you how to be more welcoming of your partner's needs.

Both of you will work on this exercise together. Read each italicized lead-in aloud, and answer the questions that follow. Decide who will go first, and swap roles when done.

Supporting partner, though you'll be facilitating the questions, you'll also be an active participant by responding to questions directed at you.

Being approachable means that when your partner is in distress, you respond warmly and show genuine concern for their well-being. *Your goal is to help soothe their in-the-moment discomfort. This might sound like "What's wrong?" or "Come, talk to me" and look like a warm embrace or sitting with them in comfortable silence.*

Recall a time when you were in distress. How did I respond?

How did it make you feel?

Is there a better way I could have responded?

Supporting partner, what do you think about the way you responded to your partner?

Supporting partner, what, if anything, would you have done differently?

Being present requires that you prioritize your partner as if they are the only person who matters in that moment. *This means that you remove all distractions by putting your phone away or turning off the TV, and you try your best not to take what they have to say personally because that moment is all about them.*

How present does it feel like I am with you?

Is there anything you think I should do to be more present?

Supporting partner, what did you get out of your partner's response?

Supporting partner, what, if anything, can you do to make yourself more present with your partner?

Being open means that you are curious about your partner's pain, and are open to supporting them in the way they need rather than giving them solutions or jumping to conclusions. *This might mean asking "How can I be helpful?" or "What do you need?" and simply using active listening to validate their concerns.*

How likely are you to talk to me about your troubles?

Recall a recent time when you tried to talk to me about a struggle you were having. How did I do?

What could I have done to support you in exactly the way you needed?

Supporting partner, what do you think about how you supported your partner in that situation?

Supporting partner, what, if anything, could you have done or said differently to support your partner in the way they needed?

The primary goal of this exercise is to show you how to create a safe environment that will encourage your partner to seek support from you, much like one that a responsive caregiver would have provided their children. However, though they make themselves fully accessible, these caregivers don't simply remove obstacles for their children. Instead, they gauge their children's capabilities and provide just enough assistance so that they're still challenged. Rather than giving them the answers, they help their children process options and find creative solutions to their struggles. The aim of these caregivers is to raise resourceful adults who are generally self-sufficient, but also able to lean on others when circumstances call for it.

On the receiving end, children feel safe to go to their caregivers when in need, and over time, develop more confidence in themselves and others to overcome difficulties. They grow up becoming confident adults who are proactive about problem solving and view relationships as a useful means to finding solutions. When dissatisfied about something, they're not afraid to initiate healthy discussions because they believe in compromise. This habit of reaching out for support ensures that whatever is making them uncomfortable will be promptly addressed.

When it comes to seeking support for problems, people tend to have the most difficulty addressing grievances directly related to the relationship. Especially if your early caregivers felt unapproachable, it's understandable for you to expect that people in general will not respond well to your grievances, and to believe it's less threatening to relationships if you don't disturb the status quo. But unresolved problems simmer and turn into bigger issues down the road, so it's crucial that you learn how to initiate difficult conversations with each other.

To increase the chances that a conversation will be productive, the most important thing to keep in mind is to prevent escalation by managing tension as much as possible. Through introspection, you have the power to influence the course of a conversation before it even starts. Introspection calls for a self-examination of your thoughts and feelings about a situation, and stems from the type of critical reasoning that a responsive caregiver might do to help their children find solutions to simple childhood problems.

When you take the time to reflect on issues, you'll have more clarity in terms of what you want to say, how you want to say it, and what you hope to get out of the conversation. This clarity improves the chances that the conversation will stay on track and increases the likelihood that you'll get your point across.

This exercise will guide you through the kinds of questions you could ask yourself to prepare for a difficult conversation with your partner. You may both work on this exercise at the same time or take turns with the book, but you'll individually write down your responses in your personal journal.

Begin by taking a moment to come up with a mild issue that you'd like to talk to your partner about. Maybe you'd like to skip their friend's birthday party, or you want to begin a monthly budget, or you'd prefer that they stop giving your children candy before dinner.

Write down this issue in your journal.

What is the goal of this conversation? In other words, what would a solution look like?

How would you benefit from having this discussion with your partner?

How has this problem been affecting you?

What do you understand about your partner's perspective of the issue?

What are you asking them to change or give up in order to work with you?

Are there any other obstacles or areas of consideration? If so, what?

What are you afraid would happen if you were to address this issue?

What would you like your partner to know about how this issue affects you? Use your feelings vocabulary to create a statement of what you can convey to your partner.

Come up with an empathic way to raise this issue with your partner, being careful not to point fingers or assign blame.

Once you've finished, you have the option of engaging your partner in a difficult conversation by sharing your responses. These prompts may help:

Share the empathic statement you created to broach this topic.

Ask, "What's your idea of a possible solution?"

Help your partner understand how this issue affects you.

This exercise was designed to recreate the kinds of internal processing you can do before addressing a sensitive topic with your partner. Your partner is much more likely to be receptive to your concerns when you approach them calmly, with a clear explanation of how you're affected by things, while also acknowledging *their* needs. To reduce the likelihood of conflict, avoid blaming or accusing, and try to open your discussions with either empathy or curiosity. For example, if you're struggling to understand your partner's perspective, you can say something like "I know you don't mean to upset me, so I want to hear what you have to say about…" The goal of these conversations is not to strong-arm your partner into accommodating your needs, but to invite them for a team discussion on how to find a solution that fits both of your needs.

Time for a Pause

We'll take a break here to give you a chance to incorporate the skills from this chapter into your routine. Over the upcoming week, continue to practice appreciating each other, staying aware of your internal processes, and working on deeper emotional discussions with each other. Specifically for this week, pay attention to how you and your partner respond to your own and each other's stress to see if you can decide what style of responsiveness the two of you gravitate toward. Once you've determined your style of responding, use the suggestions that apply to that style.

If you tend to be more self-sufficient:

- Look for signs that you're overwhelmed, and consider what you need to reactivate your PNS and bring you to a calm, logical state.
- Identify all your different stressors and categorize them. Which are most urgent? What tasks can you delegate or request help for?

If you tend to automatically seek out support:

- Look for signs that you're anxious or confused and consider what you need to reactivate your PNS so that you're in a calm, logical state.
- Identify the problem and consider what a solution might look like.
- Ask yourself: How urgently does it need to be resolved? Is it a problem that can be solved by one person? Do I have the ability to do so, even if imperfectly?

Checking In

Over the past week, you were asked to continue practicing previously learned skills, and to pay attention to ways that you respond to stress. You were given a list of self-assessment questions to contemplate before making hasty decisions on how to handle challenges. There are benefits to seeking support, and benefits to solving problems on your own, but to avoid letting your stress negatively impact your relationship, you must learn to differentiate the times you need support from the times you don't.

Engage each other in a discussion about your progress as a couple by taking turns responding to the questions below. Be thoughtful about your responses, but also don't spend too much time on them.

On a scale of 1 (dissatisfied) to 5 (very satisfied), how do you rate your relationship interactions since the last time you worked in this book?

As a team, what did you do well together this week? What can you add to your Relationship Toolbox?

If you gravitate toward being more independent, in what ways did you attempt to trust others to help? Anything you can add to your Coping Toolbox?

If you gravitate toward being more reliant on others, in what ways did you attempt to trust yourself more? Anything you can add to your Coping Toolbox?

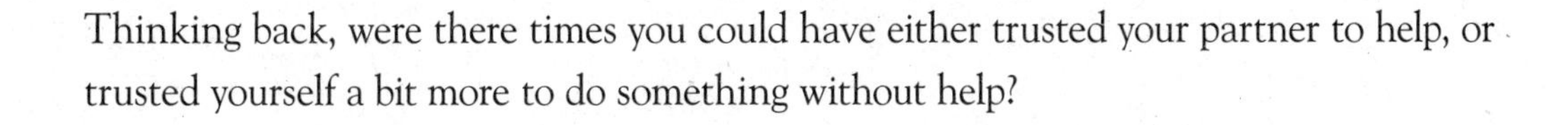

Thinking back, were there times you could have either trusted your partner to help, or trusted yourself a bit more to do something without help?

What did you learn about your partner this past week?

What's something you can do better for your relationship this upcoming week?

Share one thing your partner did this week that you appreciated.

CHAPTER 8

Warmth

Warmth is a quality of interpersonal relating that is positive, intimate, and inviting. Warm caregivers love their children very much and are generous about showing it. They desire to spend time with them, are consistently affectionate, and have a way of reassuring their children that they love them even when disappointed.

Children who receive warmth from their caregivers are able to internalize their caregivers' love, and therefore never have to question the safety of their relationship. They feel important and wanted, and trust that they would never be forgotten by their caregivers, even in each other's absence. This is important to a child's feeling of security because children need to know without doubt that somebody cares enough about them that they won't let bad things happen to them, and the love they *feel* from their caregivers reassures them of that.

But while most caregivers love their children, not all of them know how to make their children *feel* loved. By nature's design, caregivers, especially biological ones, are wired to love their children. Most of the time, children don't need to do anything for their caregivers to want to protect them, but that is not always apparent to children by the ways they're treated by their caregivers.

Caregivers who didn't receive a lot of warmth themselves may struggle to show it to their children. Generally, they present as serious, difficult to please, and cold. Though not always this way, these caregivers tend to be inconsistent with their affection, causing children to believe that love isn't a given, and there are things they must do to earn it. For example, when caregivers displace their own frustrations on their children, the children might assume they did something bad to warrant such treatment, and attempt to be "good" to deserve better treatment. Because their relationship with their caregiver fluctuates so much, they're never quite sure about how secure the relationship is. In adulthood, relationships without warmth can easily turn stale, with both partners losing motivation to bond.

Children raised by warm caregivers never needed to do anything special to feel loved because their interactions with their caregivers were consistently positive and comfortable. These caregivers were expressive about how they felt about their children and did so by being polite toward them, giving them praise, and being physically and verbally affectionate. Their caregivers actively sought out opportunities to connect with their children, such as taking family trips and spending quality time together. These pleasurable interactions led to a mutual desire for both caregiver and child to actively seek more connection with each other. As a result, these children might grow up to enjoy interpersonal bonding and seek similar methods of connecting in their adult relationships, often resulting in the creation of the kinds of pleasant relationship atmospheres that people are naturally drawn to.

What's meant by the atmosphere of a relationship is the general feeling that people have in each other's presence. In a warm caregiver–child relationship, both have a natural desire to be around each other because of the comfortable and positive feelings produced by being together. Here, the feeling of security for children comes from a feeling of certainty that their presence is not just welcome, but sought out.

As a warm caregiver would do, you and your partner can also foster a positive relationship atmosphere by being more expressive and intentional about your daily interactions with each other. Below you'll find a list of simple things you can do to enhance your relationship experience every day. Review the list with your partner, and then use the questions provided to engage each other in a guided joint discussion. Decide which of you will play which role, and swap when you reach the end of these questions.

- Compliment each other's appearance.
- Show appreciation and gratitude.
- Be polite by saying "thank you" and "excuse me."
- Give each other "just because" affection via text or a random kiss.
- Engage in playfulness by flirting or teasing each other (with kindness, of course!).
- Show genuine interest and curiosity in things your partner is interested in.
- Admire your partner by noticing and acknowledging their strengths.
- Create little inside jokes that refer to shared experiences.
- Be vocal when you see your partner doing something you like.

Supporting partner, read the questions to your partner and just listen. If it feels appropriate, try to use some of the supportive feedback skills you've been learning.

On a scale of 1 (negative) to 5 (very positive), how would you rate the atmosphere in our relationship?

From the list of positive interactions, which do you think we already do? Please provide some examples.

Which would you like to see more of?

What ideas do you have on how we can invite more positivity in our relationship?

What are the kinds of interactions that you believe hurt the atmosphere of our relationship?

How can we change that?

Humans, by nature, survive by being aware of problems, so noticing the *good* things requires conscious effort, but it doesn't take more than a slight shift in attitude to effect change in the overall vibe of your relationship. The better your partner feels around you, the stronger their natural drive to be around you.

But of course not all relationship interactions are going to be as uplifting as the ones we just talked about. What makes warm caregivers so skillful is that even when they're upset, frustrated, or disappointed in their children's behaviors, they know how to communicate in a way that doesn't make their children feel rejected or unwanted. These caregivers are not overtaken by emotional stress when their children make mistakes, and can therefore be thoughtful about the messages they send their children. On the receiving end, the consistent affection that the children receive regardless of circumstance helps them internalize their caregiver's love. In adult relationships, that unwavering affection from an early caregiver demonstrates that relationships are durable and can withstand conflicts. As a result, these individuals are unafraid to openly confront and resolve problems.

This is not the same for those who grow up with caregivers who lack warmth. When caregivers fail to show them consistent warmth, children have no evidence to gauge how their caregivers feel about them. Especially confusing are those caregivers who respond to their children's mistakes punitively. These caregivers might yell, shame, or withdraw love from their children, with the intention of reducing their undesired behavior. On the receiving end of treatment like that, children feel unloved and unwanted. Without the consistency of warm interactions to counteract feelings of occasional rejection, these children are likely to believe that relationships are fragile and therefore, will do what they can to avoid conflict.

Though avoiding conflict can protect us momentarily from losing connection with our partners, it's a bad habit that will breed resentment and break down intimacy over time. Instead of avoiding conflict, you can learn to effectively address conflicts so that your dissatisfactions don't always lead to argument. Remember that when a person feels attacked, they lose the capacity to think logically, but when problems are addressed with concern for the other person, chances for resolution significantly improve because both parties are more likely to be of sound mind.

Warm caregivers have a certain softness in the way they interact with their children, and they put thought into their communication. They are careful to avoid messages that will cause their children to feel bad about themselves, and provide specific instructions because their goal is to teach their children to do better. Though it can take practice, you can also learn to develop a more loving stance when you address problems with your partner. Particularly if you were raised in an environment where there was a lot of unfiltered dialogue, it might take some time for you to develop new language, but the more thought you put into what you say, the more successful you'll be.

A good rule of thumb to start with is to avoid words and statements that are negative. Negative communication patterns aim to punish or end an undesired behavior. The focus is typically on what's being done wrong, but unclear or vague about what's expected. These messages often carry a critical undertone that causes the receiver to feel inadequate, as if they've failed to meet your needs. Here are some examples of negative communication:

Complaining	*"You don't do anything around the house!"*
Condescension	*"I can't believe you didn't know that."*
Punishing	*Silent treatment*
Guilting	*"I would do it for you if the situation were switched!"*
Criticizing	*"You always make such a mess!"*

You could have more success by engaging in more *positive* communication patterns that aim to *add* information to help your partner better meet your needs. You can do this by first figuring out the end goal of what you're trying to say, and to directly state what you want instead.

This is what it might sound like to flip a negative message into a positive one:

Instead of complaining, communicate what you want.

"Can you help me with the dishes today?"

Instead of condescension, show them how to do it.

"Here, try it this way."

Instead of punishing, let your partner know how to correct the behavior.

"I need you to talk to me next time you spend that much."

Instead of guilting, be direct about what you want.

"I'd really appreciate it if you could stay with me."

Instead of criticizing, explain your expectation.

"When things are left around the house, it creates a lot more work for me when I'm cleaning."

Now give it a try. Below you'll find two sets of questions. In the first set, you'll show your partner how to use positive communication to share a personal complaint with you. Decide who will be the first supporting partner and who the practicing partner.

Supporting partner, read this set of questions to your partner.

Think about a time when I used a negative communication style to express a complaint to you. What do you recall me saying?

What did it feel like I was saying to you?

What do you think I was trying to communicate?

How could I have communicated it differently to you?

When the practicing partner has responded to these questions, swap roles and repeat the questions.

Once you've both completed the first set of questions, you may move on to the next set of questions, returning to the roles you initially played.

Supporting partner, this time your feedback will be requested.

What's a small complaint or frustration that you have about me?

How would you normally communicate this?

Try using positive communication to phrase the question.

Supporting partner, how did your partner do? Would you change anything about the way they stated their grievance?

Healthy communication is one way to foster warmth in your relationship, but you also have your own ideas about how to give and receive love based on what you were exposed to during childhood. While it's reasonable for you to expect to receive the kind of love that you give, it's also important to learn to give and receive love in a way that your partner is comfortable with, or else you may overlook your partner's efforts and struggle to feel satisfied.

This joint discussion exercise is designed to facilitate a conversation between you and your partner about how you both give and receive love. Decide who will go first, and swap roles when you've gone through all the questions.

Supporting partner, read the questions to your partner. Pay close attention to your partner's responses—the information will come in handy!

Take a moment to come up with a memory where you felt very loved. Describe it to me.

What does your story tell you about at least one thing that you need to feel loved?

Do I already show you love in that way? If not, how can I?

What's something else I've done to make you feel special and important?

What are the things you do for me that represent your love for me?

This chapter focused on the fifth and last emotional need that every child has to feel secure: warmth. The consistent affection that warm caregivers gave their children helped them internalize love and taught them how to foster loving environments in adulthood. As adults, these children tend to have more success in relationships; not only do they enjoy being around each other, but they also have fewer problems because they trust in the durability of their relationships and are therefore unafraid to address and resolve conflicts.

Along with the four other childhood emotional needs discussed in this book— emotional attunement, acknowledgement, unconditional acceptance, and responsiveness—you now have a set of foundational building blocks that, when practiced enough, can elevate your relationship IQ

(RQ) and help you overcome many different relationship challenges. The exercises in this chapter were designed to help you and your partner develop the kind of RQ skills that a child of an emotionally competent caregiver would have acquired, and also to keep developing your intimacy through deeper conversation and understanding of each other. My hope is that you've found some momentum to continue developing your relationship, but by no means is your work done. In fact, your work will never be done, but that just means the growth potential of your relationship is limitless.

Time for a Pause

In the next part of this workbook, you'll use the knowledge you gained to tackle common relationship obstacles, but first, let's take a break and send you off to work on integrating what we've gone over.

Continue working on the appreciation of each other, and make it a point to foster a positive atmosphere with each other. Pay attention to your internal processes and the dialogue in your head, and be thoughtful about ways that you communicate and engage with your partner. Use your emotional vocabulary to improve articulating your feelings and needs, and be curious about your partner's emotional experiences too. More specifically for this week, I'd like you to pay attention to your treatment of each other by doing the following:

- Using what you learned about ways your partner experiences love, come up with at least one way you can show them love the way they best receive it.
- Try to catch yourself before you use negative communication, and ask yourself whether what you're about to say is necessary. If it is, think about less hurtful ways to get your message across.
- Notice when you feel positive around your partner and make it known to them. Try to vocalize what it is about the moment that makes you feel connected.

Checking In

Your assignment over the past week was to work on inviting more warmth into your relationship by replacing negative statements with positive ones. You were also asked to pay attention to the ways that you both give and receive love in your relationship, and to incorporate that knowledge more into your interactions with each other.

Engage each other in a discussion about your progress as a couple by taking turns responding to the questions below. Be thoughtful about your responses, but also don't spend too much time on them.

On a scale of 1 (dissatisfied) to 5 (very satisfied), how do you rate your relationship interactions since the last time you worked in this workbook?

In what ways were the two of you successful in trying to foster a more positive relationship this week?

What are the RQ tools that you think you're excelling in? What about your partner?

Which RQ tools are you struggling with? What about your partner?

In what ways has working on this book changed the way you relate to each other?

What's something you can do better for your relationship this upcoming week?

Share one thing your partner did this week that you appreciated.

Applying Relationship Skills

If you've made it this far without skipping any chapters, it's likely that you've added some useful skills to your existing relationship IQ (RQ) skill set and, hopefully, begun a journey toward a secure and fulfilling relationship.

I want to remind you that the goal after completing this workbook is not to have a "perfect" relationship free of conflict, but to learn to work through challenges in a way that will ultimately deepen your intimacy and elevate your relationship experience. Because we humans are complicated beings and sensitive to the constant changes in our environments, learning to navigate your relationship is an ongoing process that will never be complete. That's why this book does not aim to solve all of your relationship challenges, but instead it provides you a set of foundational tools that will help you and your partner build a substantive relationship. My hope is that with enough practice, each challenge you overcome will add to your confidence, as a couple, in your ability to resolve whatever obstacles the uncertain future brings. That is the emotional security we all seek.

Depending on where you are in your relationship journey, this may all sound too idealistic. Some people might worry that this work will take away from the familiar relationship they've already built together. Perhaps the practices thus far have felt scripted or artificial, and you're afraid that you'll lose the comfort of being spontaneous in your relationship. And though free expression should be part of every healthy relationship, it's useless if your message doesn't get across the way you intend. The intention of this workbook is primarily to help you enhance your existing relationship by helping you develop tools to clearly comprehend and accurately meet each other's needs.

As with anything new, these skills take time to mature and need to be practiced consistently before they become part of your relationship habits. Expect it to feel awkward at first, expect to need to use this workbook for reference, and expect to struggle through it. In fact, you may logically understand the concepts behind the tools covered in this book, but that's different from knowing how to integrate them into your existing relationship. That's why I've dedicated the last part of this book solely to showing you how and in what situations to apply your RQ tools.

In chapter 9, we'll review each of the five emotional needs one by one, and take a look at how they can be applied to everyday interactions. You'll find vignette exercises that illustrate common communication mistakes couples make, and you'll be challenged to use your RQ skills to find better ways to work through the issues. Additionally, you'll be asked to engage each other in exercises related to topics surrounding your own relationship, and you can use those exercises as a reference to guide you through issues should you need to do so in the future. Because most conflicts begin due to either lack of communication or poor communication, this section is going to be useful in helping to avoid those close calls to arguing and redirecting you on a path toward resolution.

Though the objective of chapter 9 is to help you improve communication and thereby reduce the occurrence of frustrating arguments, you'll still inevitably get into disagreements that are upsetting. As effective as some of these RQ tools may be, there will be times under high amounts of pressure when you either consciously or subconsciously decide that you don't want to do the work. And *that's okay*. That's what chapter 10 is for.

In our final chapter, you'll learn how to get past an argument and make up in a way that doesn't just restore your relationship, but also strengthens it. There's a common misconception that too much fighting is a sign of a "bad" relationship, but that's not always true, especially if you know how to work through your differences. The contents of chapter 10 will show you how your RQ tools can come together to support your relationship's most difficult moments. But before we do that, let's see what your newly developed RQ tools can do to help the two of you manage those pesky little interactions that can ruin an otherwise enjoyable moment together.

CHAPTER 9

Using Relationship IQ Tools to Work Through Issues

I've lost count of the number of times I've heard a person say, "When things are good, they're *really* good," about their partnership. As nice as it is to appreciate the connection you feel when things are harmonious, the true measure of a healthy relationship is how the two of you, as a couple, work through the *not-so-good* times. I've already alluded to it many times, but I cannot stress enough how detrimental unresolved conflict can be for your relationship. This is because your unmet needs don't simply disappear, they break down intimacy, block your chances at reaching emotional security, and will surface in the least productive moments when you're tired of pretending that things don't bother you. If you don't learn to get past those bad times, then unfortunately, your good times will be numbered.

To effectively overcome difficulties both partners must work collaboratively, and what makes this challenging is that despite your common goal for a harmonious relationship, you each also have matters of individual importance that you'll fight to protect. So especially when personal needs or values clash, you must find a way to talk about what's important to you without dismissing what's important to your partner.

Many people simply don't know how to go about this effectively, and either lean too far to the aggressive side or simply surrender to keep the peace. When either of those happens, the road to resolution becomes inaccessible because you're either both fighting to protect your own interests, or pretending there's not a problem when there is.

While there's nothing wrong with self-advocating, if your goal is to be part of a secure and lasting relationship, then you should always be on the same team as your partner, with a goal of prioritizing the interests of the relationship. When there are differences, you must both be willing to momentarily set aside your position to try and see things through your partner's perspective, because usually the solution lies somewhere in between.

As uncomfortable as it can be to bring up topics of disagreement, it's how you clear the path to build a strong intimate connection with your partner. Though many people struggle with it, getting past disagreements with your partner is not that huge a task once you get better at managing emotions. There are ways to broach sensitive topics without the situation becoming contentious. What makes it difficult is that, when triggered, your fight-or-flight system can easily set off your partner's. Just the way animals can sense fear in other animals and trigger a bloody fight for survival, you and your partner are also sensitive to each other's moods and can easily jump into defensive action in a fraction of a second.

The secret is in learning to steer those fight-or-flight moments so that they don't detract from the original issue, which can be done by using your relationship IQ (RQ) tools to either prevent or manage emotionally charged exchanges. In chapters 4–8, you began to practice and develop healthy relationship tools, but you must also know when and how to effectively apply them to your relationship exchanges.

This chapter is divided into five sections that will each provide a brief overview of an emotional need, followed by sample exercises illustrating common relationship interactions that you'll work through using RQ tools.

You'll notice that the organization of this chapter is going to be a little different. Rather than completing the entire chapter in one sitting, I recommend that you split the five sections up into five separate sessions. You're welcome to decide how frequently you work on this chapter, but I highly recommend that you allow at least two days between the workbook sessions. Though the sections are short, the work is just as important because it's meant to deepen your practice of what you've already learned. At the end of each section, you'll find suggestions on different ways you can mindfully apply the skills in your interactions with your partner. Let's take a look.

Emotional Attunement

When our partners are emotionally attuned to us, they're able to temporarily suspend their own feelings about a situation and instead, imagine themselves in our position. When they do this, they're better able to recognize the legitimacy of our feelings, which creates a safe environment for us to be vulnerable about our needs.

Having the freedom to honestly express our feelings and needs greatly improves our chances of finding peace because, as humans, we're built to feel uncomfortable until our unmet needs are tended to. So if you want your partner to provide you this safe space, you must be able to do the same for them.

Emotionally attuning to your partner means that you dedicate yourself to recognizing and understanding their feelings so that you can become an ally in helping them meet their needs. This can be done by paying attention to and correctly interpreting their verbal and nonverbal cues, using the contexts of a situation to empathize with their pain, and encouraging more vulnerability by validating their experiences.

By tuning into each other's emotions that way, you gradually develop a deeper mutual understanding that helps the two of you meet each other's needs in ways that nobody else can.

Here are a few examples of circumstances where you can use emotional attunement to assess a situation, create safety, or connect on a deeper level:

- When your partner is stressed or overwhelmed about something
- When your partner has a complaint
- When an argument is starting to escalate
- When you want to find the right time to bring something up
- When you want to communicate how you feel
- When your partner is celebrating an achievement and you want to join them

The following vignette exercise illustrates what emotionally attuning to your partner's feelings could look like. The questions that follow the story focus on learning how to use emotional attunement to empathize and validate another person's feelings.

Select one partner to read the story aloud.

Fabio and Geo are on their first overseas vacation together since they began dating a year ago. Geo is an avid traveler, and initiated the trip because Fabio had never left the country before. He hopes that this trip will introduce Fabio to the joys of traveling so they can do it more together.

Fabio grew up shy and sheltered. He appreciates how outgoing Geo is, but often turns down Geo's suggestions to do more outdoorsy things because he's insecure about his lack of athleticism. However, due to the increasing trust the two have been building, Fabio has recently been more open to trying new adventures with Geo, which Geo hopes to take full advantage of on this trip.

On the morning of their second day on vacation, Geo suggested that the two rent bikes to tour the surrounding cities. With some reassurance from Geo that they'd avoid riding in crowded places, Fabio reluctantly agreed.

The first ten minutes of the bike ride was smooth. Fabio was gradually becoming more comfortable on the bike, and was enjoying the wind in his face. Suddenly, without warning, the narrow road they were on emptied into a main street packed with tourists and street vendors. Fabio panicked, and all he could see was Geo getting farther away. Trying hard to maneuver between a crowd of tourists, Fabio fell off his bike and landed in the middle of the road. Fabio was red in the face and looked up to see Geo rushing toward him.

Geo: Oh no! Are you okay?

Fabio: Get away from me, you liar! You don't care about me!

Geo: I was just trying to check on you! Why are you being so dramatic?

Fabio: I told you I haven't ridden a bike in ages! How was I supposed to get past all those people?

Geo: I wasn't even going that fast!

Fabio: I don't want to do this anymore. Let's just go back to the hotel!

Now, respond to these questions separately, each in your own journal.

What do you think about the dialogue that occurred between Geo and Fabio?

Where do you think the first break in communication occurred? What was wrong with it?

Based on the context, and Fabio's verbal and nonverbal cues, what do you think Fabio was feeling when he rejected Geo's efforts?

Rather than rejecting Geo's efforts, what might it have sounded like if Fabio had used words to communicate how he felt in that moment?

How do you think Geo felt when he was rushing toward Fabio?

What do you think about Geo's response to Fabio's rejection of his concern?

How do you think Geo's responses made Fabio feel?

What's something more validating that Geo could have said to Fabio to empathize with his situation?

Once you've completed the questions on your own, review your individual responses with your partner, then work together to come up with a joint response for each question before moving on.

This exercise was designed to help the two of you reflect upon how attuning to your partner's in-the-moment emotions can soothe a tense situation and guide you toward deeper understanding. Each time you and your partner demonstrate understanding of each other's feelings, you foster a safer environment for honest and open communication.

Here's an example of how empathy and validation might sound to change the direction of the dialogue:

Geo: Oh no! Are you okay?

Fabio: Get away from me, you liar! You don't care about me!

Geo: I get why you're upset. You must feel embarrassed and disappointed in me because I promised that I would take care of you.

On top of managing conflict, you can also use your attunement skills to support your partner through difficult times. Here's a simple exercise to help you attune to your partner when they're having a hard time.

Decide which of you will go first, and swap roles when the exercise is completed.

Supporting partner, you'll play a more active role this time. Rather than facilitating the exercise, you'll use your active listening skills to pay close attention to your partner's story, and try to imagine what they might be thinking or feeling. After your partner finishes sharing their story, you'll answer the questions below to help you empathize with your partner's difficulty.

Practicing partner, give yourself some time to come up with a stressful experience you had to deal with in the last week or two. After you have a situation in mind, share with your partner what happened.

Supporting partner, pay attention to your partner's story and respond to the following questions after your partner is finished sharing.

Do you need your partner to clarify anything? Any additional information that you want to know about your partner's story?

In your own words, briefly summarize what you understand about your partner's story. Check with your partner if you missed anything.

What, if any, verbal or nonverbal cues did your partner display while sharing their story that could inform you of how they were feeling while sharing?

Imagine yourself in your partner's position. How might they be feeling? What might they be thinking? Complete the following sentence to validate your partner's experience: *If I were you, I would feel ______________, and think ______________.*

What do you think your partner needs to feel better? If you don't know, feel free to ask your partner questions like:

"Is there anything I can do for you?"

"What do you need?"

"How can I be helpful?"

"In what way would you like me to support you?"

This last exercise is an example of how you might try to understand your partner by emotionally attuning to them. It's a common misconception that the way to tend to a loved one's struggles is to solve their problems, but most of the time, all they want is for somebody to listen and validate their feelings. Couples who empathize with each other feel more secure because their level of understanding of each other is unrivaled by anybody else in their lives.

Time for a Pause

Give yourselves a couple of days to continue working on attunement. To truly connect with your partner, pay attention to the meaning behind their words, their facial expressions, and the circumstances surrounding their struggle, and ask yourself, "If I were in their position, how would I feel? What would I think?" Should you feel the need, bookmark this page and use it as a reference for future times when you want to support your partner.

Acknowledgment

When your partner acknowledges you, they honor you as a worthy individual with valid feelings and perspectives whether those align with theirs or not. They value your opinions and include you in their decisions, especially the ones pertaining to the relationship.

When we're included in decisions, we feel valued as equal contributors to the relationship, and that gives us some sense of control over the things that happen to us, as well as a sense of worthiness in the relationship. We must always remember that our partners also need the same level of acknowledgment from us.

The way you go about honoring your partner's differences is by always valuing their contributions no matter how big or small. Especially if you were raised by caregivers who didn't value children's opinions, you should pay attention to ways that *you* approach decision making in relationships. When you struggle to make sense of your partner's perspectives, keep an open mind, and try to proceed with curiosity rather than condemnation or dismissal. When important decisions need to be made, embrace the idea that two heads are often better than one by including their opinions and feedback.

Here are examples of common situations where you can use acknowledgment of your partner's differences to promote more collaborative problem solving:

- When you have opposing opinions about something
- When you need to make big decisions that will affect both of you
- When you develop new routines for the relationship

- When you need help solving a difficult personal dilemma
- When your partner tries to share a part of their life with you
- When your partner starts a conversation on a topic you're passionate about

The following vignette exercise will help illustrate what acknowledging your partner's perspectives could look like. Questions that follow the story will focus on helping you come up with ways to invite more collaborative discussions that respect each other's perspectives.

Decide who will read the story aloud, and respond to the corresponding questions separately in your own journal. Once you've answered all of the questions on your own, rejoin your partner. Engage in a joint discussion by first sharing your individual responses, and then work together to see if you can both come up with something better.

Singh and Judee have been dating for about a year and recently started saving money to get married. Though their values have generally aligned, they continue to clash on one big topic: money. Judee and Singh frequently disagree on how much to spend on various expenses.

Having grown up in poverty, Singh understands the value of hard work. He recalls working odd jobs and how receiving good tips used to make up for all the grief that rude customers would put him through. Now that he's established, he tries to provide the same moral encouragement to service workers by tipping generously.

Judee, on the other hand, was raised by immigrant parents who rose out of poverty through hard work and frugal spending. Although her family was considered part of the upper-middle class by the time she was born, her parents continued to instill the values of budgeting and taught her to make smart money decisions by not spending frivolously. Thanks to their guidance, Judee was able to purchase her first home when she was just twenty-six years old, which reinforced to her that she made good money decisions.

On one particular evening out, Singh and Judee finished dinner, and after they paid for valet parking, they both watched the attendant run twenty feet away to retrieve the car. When the attendant pulled up in front of them, Singh tipped him the amount of the cost of parking. As the two drove off, their exchange went like this:

Judee: I can't believe you tipped him so much for doing absolutely nothing!

Singh: I knew you were going to complain about that!

Judee: It's just stupid! Don't you see that they're just trying to swindle you?

Singh: I can do whatever I want. It's my money!

Judee: We're supposed to be working together to save money!

Singh: Then maybe we shouldn't get married!

Working separately, reflect on these questions and respond to them in your own journal.

What do you think about the dialogue that occurred between Singh and Judee?

Where do you think the first break in communication occurred? What was wrong with it?

What do you think about how Judee approached Singh?

How do you think that must have made Singh feel?

What was it about her values that drove Judee's reaction to Singh's tipping?

How could Judee have responded differently to invite a more collaborative discussion with Singh about his tipping?

What do you understand about Singh's values that drove his decision to tip so generously?

How could Singh have responded differently to invite a more collaborative discussion with Judee?

Before moving on, share your responses with each other and work together to see if you can come up with better answers.

This vignette exercise illustrated a pretty common example of how many disagreements start between couples. One person does something the other disagrees with, setting up a back-and-forth where both insist their way of doing things is the correct way.

Here's what it could have sounded like if Judee had tried to be more acknowledging of Singh's perspectives:

Judee: I personally would never tip that much for somebody to do so little. Can you help me understand your logic?

Singh: I get why it's hard for you to understand. When I see these guys out here hustling, it reminds me of myself, and I just want to reward them for trying.

Judee: I see what you're saying. I guess I only saw the value of the work, and I appreciate your kindness.

The truth is, there's never just one way to do or view things, and you must make room for your partner's ideas to exist in your relationship. Here's a brief exercise to walk you through how the two of you can manage your differences. Decide who will play what role first, and then swap roles and repeat the exercise.

Supporting partner, your partner will be asked to discuss a topic, and your job is to use your active listening skills to pay close attention to their story. The goal here is not about *agreeing* with your partner, but to at least see the logic in their perspectives. When they've finished their story, there will be a set of questions that you'll facilitate.

Practicing partner, take a moment to come up with something that frustrates you about your partner. Maybe you don't see eye-to-eye about a particular individual or you don't like the way they do a certain chore. Tell your partner how you feel about this topic and why it bothers you so much.

Supporting partner, pay attention to your partner's story and respond to the following questions after your partner has finished sharing.

What's your perspective on your partner's chosen topic?

Briefly summarize the important points your partner shared and check with them to see if you missed anything.

After listening to your partner's explanation, do you fully see the logic behind their perspective?

If so, what's a new viewpoint that you now have?

If not, what else do you need to know from your partner to better understand their perspective? These deepening questions might help:

- *What is personal to you about this topic?*
- *What was your first exposure to this topic?*
- *What personal values surround this topic?*
- *Why do you feel so strongly about this topic?*
- *What does this topic represent for you?*

These two exercises are designed to help you create a more collaborative relationship with your partner. Couples acknowledging each other's individual worth leads to strong relationship security. Each time you make room for your partner's perspectives, *they* feel more secure in knowing that they add value to the relationship, and *you* feel secure in trusting that you can lean on them to fill your gaps in knowledge and comprehension of the world.

Time for a Pause

I'd like to suggest you take a break here. You can continue to practice acknowledging your partner by reminding yourself that there's *always* value and rationale behind their contributions, and dedicating yourself to fully understanding them deeply. If you find that you sometimes struggle to make space for your partner, I encourage you to bookmark this last exercise and follow the question prompts to help you better appreciate your partner's perspectives.

Unconditional Acceptance

When we experience unconditional acceptance from somebody, that means that they are committed to us as we are, without any agenda. Rather than expecting us to fit their narratives of what they want in a partner, they accept the reality of who we are.

Having freedom to be comfortable in your own skin relieves you from the pressures of needing to be somebody you're not. When your partner shows you unconditional acceptance, you're free to be your most natural self and share your most honest feelings, thus increasing the chances that your deepest needs are heard and addressed. This is a need that your partner also has, and you can offer them the same by letting go of the ways you think things *should* be, and trusting that you can find happiness with them, imperfections and all.

You can work on showing acceptance of your partner by seeing them as a whole person rather than judging them by their shortcomings. Particularly if you were raised around a lot of negative criticism, pay attention to the way you respond to your partner when they do or say something that doesn't sit well with you. When they make mistakes, show concern for their struggle and provide opportunity to right their wrong. By demonstrating acceptance of each other, you foster a safe environment for both to show up authentically as individuals, so you can use each other's strengths and weaknesses to co-create a relationship tailored toward both of your specific needs.

Here are several examples of the types of circumstances where unconditional acceptance can apply:

- When you need to let go of unrealistic relationship expectations
- When you need to forgive your partner for mistakes or wrongdoings
- When you can't find a middle ground and need to negotiate a solution that works for both
- When you want to understand your partner's struggles more deeply
- When you want to shift focus away from your partner's flaws and appreciate their strengths

The following vignette exercise will walk you through what unconditional acceptance could look like when two imperfect people enter a relationship with each other. Questions that follow the story will be directed at helping you accept and work with the fundamental differences between you and your partner.

Read the story aloud together, and respond to the corresponding questions separately in your own journal. Once you've answered all of the questions on your own, rejoin your partner and engage in a joint discussion by first sharing your individual responses with each other, and then work together to see if you can both come up with something better.

Yumi and Jack have been married for just over three years. Though they generally have a good relationship, one source of ongoing disagreement surrounds Yumi's social life.

Yumi was raised an only child by two hardworking parents. Because her parents were always busy, Yumi kept herself busy by being around friends. As an adult, she looks forward to filling her weekends with social events, and has been wanting to integrate Jack into her group of friends for years.

Though Jack has developed some close relationships with certain friends of Yumi's, he feels that he sees them too much. Growing up the middle child of five children, Jack was always around people, which he found somewhat exhausting at times, and he would often retreat to his own room to read. As an adult, Jack has a handful of very close friends that he keeps in touch with primarily via texting or occasional dinners. He much prefers to spend quality time with Yumi in the comfort of their home.

Over lunch one Saturday afternoon, Jack and Yumi were discussing what they should do that evening. Their conversation went like this:

Jack: What about bowling tonight? There's that new place that opened nearby.

Yumi: Oh yeah! I'll call Becca and Craig!

Jack: I was really hoping it would just be the two of us this time…

Yumi: Why do you always have to be so antisocial?

Jack: We just saw your friends last week!

Yumi: What's wrong with that?

Separately, reflect on these questions and respond in your journal:

What are your initial thoughts about the dialogue that occurred between Yumi and Jack?

What do you see as the main problem here?

What does Jack's opposition to inviting Yumi's friends suggest about who Jack is and what he needs?

What do you understand about who Yumi is, and what she wants from Jack?

How do you think Jack must have felt when Yumi called him antisocial?

If Yumi were to accept the reality of who Jack is, what adjustments should she make in terms of her expectations of him?

Before moving on, share your responses with each other and work together to see if you can come up with better answers.

No matter how many similarities you and your partner have, you'll undoubtedly have differences that can disturb the peace in your relationship. This vignette exercise provides an example of the types of personality clashes couples commonly deal with. When you struggle to accept parts of your partner, they're likely to feel as though there's something wrong with them, which may even lead to harmful consequences like dishonesty and resentment.

Here's an example of what it could look like for Yumi to show a bit more acceptance of Jack's preferences:

Jack: What about bowling tonight? There's that new place that opened nearby.

Yumi: Oh yeah! I'll call up my friends!

Jack: I was really hoping it would just be the two of us this time…

Yumi: You're usually so willing to spend time with my friends, and I know that can be a lot for you sometimes. Let's just go me and you tonight. That'll be fun for both of us.

Showing acceptance of your partner's differences does not mean that you support or align with them, but it does mean that you'll try to work with your partner and not make them feel bad about themself. Here's an exercise that can help you use unconditional acceptance to make room for the both of you to be more authentic in your relationship.

Decide who will play what role first, and then swap roles and repeat the exercise after.

Supporting partner, your partner will be asked to be vulnerable about a topic, and your job is to create a safe space by listening with compassion. Invest your energy into showing concern for their struggle and avoid any feedback that may come off negative or judgmental. When their story is finished, there will be a set of questions for you to facilitate.

Practicing partner, take a moment to think about something you've been trying to hide from your partner. This might be a bad habit, like smoking cigarettes, or a complaint you've hesitated to address. If it helps, use the Share-Check-Share technique you previously learned. You may begin whenever you're ready.

Supporting partner, after your partner has finished sharing, answer the following questions out loud:

- In your own words, what has your partner been concealing from you?
- What do you understand about why your partner hasn't been direct about this issue?
- In what ways do you think you could have contributed to making your partner feel unsafe to share this?

(Check in with your partner, and ask whether there are other reasons they were afraid to share this in the past.)

- What's your understanding of how your partner has been affected by not being able to be transparent about this part of their life? *(If you're not sure, ask for clarification.)*

- What would you need to let go of in order to accept this part of your partner?

Now that the two of you have a deeper understanding of each other's perspectives, work together to come up with some possible solutions where both person's needs are equally considered. Is there a middle ground? Is this issue just something you must accept?

The last two exercises you completed were designed to promote a more harmonious relationship in spite of your differences. Because you and your partner are unique individuals, you'll undoubtedly encounter clashes in personality, values, and expectations. However, rather than harming your relationship, each disagreement can also be viewed as an opportunity to remove another obstacle toward deeper intimacy. The goal is to learn to accept the reality of who you both are, and find ways to either incorporate or work around each other's differences. Through mutual acceptance of each other, you can both show up as your most natural selves. The result is the security of knowing that there's nobody else that you can be as vulnerable with other than your chosen partner.

Time for a Pause

Take a couple of days after this section to work on unconditional acceptance. If it helps, you can refer back to this last exercise to help explore solutions each time you and your partner encounter differences that you're struggling to move past.

Responsiveness

Responsive partners are accessible and emotionally present. They are concerned about their partner's well-being and committed to finding ways to ease their distress. Because of this, they maintain warm and welcoming attitudes, and strive to make their loved ones feel comfortable.

On the receiving end, we feel safe in multiple ways. The fact that our partner is so accessible reassures us that we can always count on them to help us out of binds, no matter where or when. Their gentle demeanor makes us feel safe to approach them with concerns, whether our grievances are personal or pertaining to the relationship. This ensures that problems will be promptly addressed and not continue to burden the relationship over time.

You can foster such an environment for your partner and encourage more inter-dependency by making yourself accessible to them. Depending on your caregiver's level of responsiveness, it's possible that you now struggle to respond to others' needs in a way that feels helpful, which can discourage your partner from coming to you for help when there's a problem. To be a more supportive partner, pay attention to the ways you respond to your partner's efforts to connect or ask for help from you. This doesn't mean that you must neglect your life to tend to theirs, but you can learn to respond to their needs warmly, even if you're unable to tend to them. When they share troubles, even when they're about you, stay empathic by focusing attention on *their* concerns rather than defending yourself. Trust that you'll have a chance to state your case later.

Here are examples of situations where you can practice more positive responsiveness toward your partner:

- When your partner has a bad day
- When your partner is excited about a new venture or achievement
- When your partner has an urgent favor they need to ask of you
- When your partner suffers a loss of any kind
- When you notice your partner reacting more strongly than expected
- When your partner complains about somebody you care about

The following vignette exercise illustrates a common exchange that can go wrong when one partner responds poorly to their partner's need for support. Questions that follow the story will be focused on helping you use RQ skills to respond in a way that can gradually encourage more reliance on each other over time.

Read the story aloud together, and respond to the corresponding questions separately in your own journal. Once you've answered all of the questions on your own, rejoin your partner and engage in a joint discussion by first sharing your individual responses with each other, and then work together to see if you can both come up with something better.

Chester and Malaya have been married for six years. Throughout the time they've been together, Malaya has spent most of her weekends traveling an hour away with Chester to visit his family. Because Chester is very close to his family, making frequent visits to see them was the compromise that Malaya made with him in order to live slightly closer to her own friends and family.

Recently, Malaya was promoted at work, which meant longer hours in the office, so she was really starting to look forward to relaxing on the weekends. Though Malaya always enjoyed spending time with her in-laws, she suddenly found herself resistant to going and was noticeably less engaged when she was with them. Malaya recognized that she probably needed more time to rest at home during the weekends, but she didn't want to be unfair to Chester because of their previous agreement. To not go back on her word, Malaya continued accompanying her husband to see his family, but she began building some resentment over going.

One evening on their drive home, Malaya summoned up the courage to initiate the following conversation:

Malaya: Hey, there's something that's been on my mind…

Chester: What's up? I could tell you were withdrawn today.

Malaya: It's been a lot coming all the way here to see your family every weekend. I really didn't want to come today, but I felt like I had to.

Chester: So you're trying to go back on your word then? We had a deal!

Malaya: No! That's not what I'm trying to say!

Chester: So what now? Do you not want to come with me anymore?

Malaya: Forget it…

Now, respond to these questions separately, each in your own journal.

What do you think about the dialogue that happened?

Where do you think the first break in communication occurred?

What could have been said or done differently?

What was Malaya's goal for initiating the conversation with Chester?

What do you think about how Chester responded to Malaya?

How do you think Chester's response made Malaya feel?

How else could Chester have responded to make Malaya feel safer to continue sharing her concerns?

If Chester could empathize with how Malaya felt, what's something validating he could have said to her?

Before moving on, share your responses with each other and work together to see if you can come up with better answers.

The dialogue in this exercise depicts how difficult conversations can sometimes get shut down. The struggling partner was already hesitant to raise the issue, and the receiving partner's defensive reaction further reinforced the struggling partner's initial fears. Here's what it might sound like if Chester were to be more responsive to Malaya's feelings:

Malaya: Hey, there's something that's been on my mind…

Chester: What's up? I could tell you were withdrawn today.

Malaya: It's been a lot coming all the way here to see your family every weekend. I really didn't want to come today, but I felt like I had to.

Chester: I get that it can be a lot, and I appreciate you being willing to come with me all the time. Why the sudden change?

To create the right conditions that'll encourage your partner to open up to you, a good rule of thumb is to detach yourself from the story and try to position yourself as a concerned parent attending to their precious child. The next exercise will walk you through steps you can take to be a safe source of support for your partner.

Decide who will play the supporting partner first and who the practicing partner. Then swap roles and repeat the exercise.

Supporting partner, your partner will be sharing a sensitive topic with you, and your job is to follow the prompts to guide you through supporting your partner. Your goal here is to create a safe space to encourage your partner to open up to you. Refer back to chapter 7 for assistance if necessary.

Practicing partner, you'll be asked by your partner to share a difficulty. It can be about your partner, your relationship, or something else. At any point, if you begin to feel uncomfortable or the conversation takes a wrong turn, you can ask your partner to stop the exercise. Come up with a topic to share, and let your partner know when they can begin asking the questions that follow.

How do you feel about what you're about to share?

Supporting partner, say something warm and reassuring to ease your partner's discomfort, and invite them to share their concern with you. (*Use your active listening skills and try to comprehend the significance of what your partner is trying to tell you.*)

Supporting partner, in your own words, what do you understand about what your partner needs help with? (*Check in with your partner and ask if you understood them correctly, and whether there's anything they would like to clarify.*)

Supporting partner, try to empathize with your partner, and validate their feelings. Complete this sentence if you're having trouble coming up with another sentence starter: "If I were you, I would feel _______________."

Supporting partner, ask your partner an open-ended question to begin exploring ways you can be helpful. Here are some ideas of things you could say:

"How can I be helpful?"

"What do you need?"

"What ideas do you have to resolve this?"

"What might a solution look like?"

The two exercises in this section are designed to help the two of you foster a more interdependent relationship, allowing you to lean on each other during difficult times. Couples who turn to each other for help tend to have more relationship security; they benefit not only from receiving support but also from feeling valued for giving support.

Time for a Pause

This could be a good place to pause. To continue building interdependence when you feel overwhelmed, you can confide in your partner for emotional support, and work with them to see if there's anything they can do to help lessen your burdens. Work on building awareness of the ways in which you respond to your partner when they seek support from you, and remind yourself to be gentle, even if you're unable to offer the help they seek. If you find yourself struggling to be supportive, refer back to the second exercise in this section and use it to guide you if necessary.

Warmth

Partners who are warm tend to be naturally positive, trusting, and affectionate. They generally try to see others in a positive light, and believe that people are inherently good. Because they like people, they value togetherness, they're polite toward others, and they never hesitate to show love.

On the receiving end, we feel comfortable with a warm partner and never have to question their love for us. Their respectful demeanor toward others means that they are likable, not quick to take things personally, and seldomly end up in conflict with others. We feel safe to be ourselves around them, and don't frequently have to watch what we do or say. People like this are easy to be around, and we feel naturally motivated to be in their presence.

For your partner, it feels good for them to know that you *naturally* desire being around them. You can also promote such an atmosphere for your partner by trying to focus your attention on their positive traits, and by making deliberate efforts to show them love. In conversations, you can try to be agreeable, which doesn't mean agreeing with everything they're saying, but staying mindful of what the tone and delivery of your responses convey. If you weren't raised in a very warm environment, you may at times find yourself craving affection, but being afraid to show or ask for it. If your early caregivers were critical, judgmental, or untrusting, it's possible that you may have developed a generally negative perception of others. Such a view of others can pollute your relationship and create tense and adversarial dynamics that a person would naturally want to avoid.

These are examples of opportunities where you can inject more warmth through positive compliments or affection:

- When you feel taken care of
- When your partner *finally* makes the change you've been asking for
- When you experience a moment of gratitude for them
- When they handle a situation well
- When they show personal growth in something
- When they are having a bad day
- When the two of you are disagreeing on a topic

The following vignette exercise depicts a fairly common example of how a normal conversation can escalate into an argument when there's no warmth in the relationship. Questions that follow the story will help you use positive warmth to drive more meaningful discussions.

Read the story aloud together, and respond to the corresponding questions separately in your own journal. Once you've answered all of the questions on your own, rejoin your partner and engage in a joint discussion by first sharing your individual responses with each other, and then work together to see if you can both come up with something better.

Alexus and Julio are newlyweds, but were together for about eight years before tying the knot. Though Alexus had been wanting to settle down three years into their relationship, they decided to wait until Julio was ready because he had a lot to work through from his last relationship.

Prior to meeting Alexus, Julio had ended a six-year relationship with an ex-fiancée because he discovered that she had been in a second relationship throughout most of the time they were together. Julio had put all of his trust into this person and was devastated after the breakup. He wasn't sure if he could ever trust anybody again.

Luckily, Julio was able to fall in love again when he met Alexus, a person who had a lot of integrity and was well-liked by others. Alexus's longest relationship prior to Julio had lasted only two years, and also ended due to her partner's infidelity. Though Alexus was able to get over the betrayal, she was also empathic to Julio's traumatic breakup, and therefore willing to be patient about marriage.

One evening, the two were watching a reality TV show where a woman accused her partner of cheating because he was flirting with strangers at a bar, which prompted this discussion:

Julio: Wow…what a jerk. Once a cheater, always a cheater.

Alexus: You consider that cheating?

Julio: Of course it's cheating. He's flirting with somebody while he's in a relationship with another person!

Alexus: I mean, I don't think what he did is acceptable, but I don't really consider that *cheating.*

Julio: Are you kidding me? This is just common sense!

Now, respond to these questions separately, each in your own journal.

What do you think about this exchange between Alexus and Julio?

How do you feel about Julio's general demeanor in his first statement?

How would it feel to be part of a conversation like this?

If Julio were to try to be more warm and nonjudgmental, how else could he have delivered his initial comment?

What do you think about Alexus's follow-up question: "You consider that cheating?"

Why do you think Julio had such a strong reaction?

What is Julio insinuating about Alexus when he says things like "Are you kidding me? This is just common sense!"

How else could Julio have engaged Alexus so as not to shut down the conversation?

Before moving on, share your responses with each other and work together to see if you can come up with better answers.

This exchange between Julio and Alexus illustrates how a casual conversation can turn tense. One partner makes an extreme comment that's questioned or opposed by the other, and triggers an unsavory back-and-forth that ruins an otherwise bonding experience. You can learn to avoid this type of unnecessary friction by engaging in polite dialogue, and paying attention to harsh undertones that serve to dominate or be "right." Conversation between couples is an important tool in getting to know each other, and leads to deeper intimacy over time.

Here's an example of how Julio could have approached the conversation in a more loving way:

Julio: Wow…to me, that's cheating. What do you think?

Alexus: I don't know. I don't agree with his actions, but I personally think cheating is more than that.

Julio: Maybe I'm more sensitive to it because of my past. I admire how you've been able to move past being cheated on.

Alexus: Well, I think your situation was a lot more traumatic because you were going to get married.

To have more meaningful conversations with each other, try to keep in mind that people who care about you *never* intend to hurt you. If you do feel triggered by something they say, ask yourself, "What is my partner trying to say if I assume that they don't have bad intentions?" The next exercise will give you ideas of how to deepen your intimacy simply by being warm and positive in your daily conversations with each other.

Decide who will play what role first, then swap roles and repeat the exercise when the first part is done.

Supporting partner, your partner will share an experience with you, and your job is to try and relate to what they're saying in a warm and positive way. Prompts will be provided to guide you through the conversation as well as suggested questions you can ask to deepen the discussion. Work on the delivery of your messages by thinking about what you say before you say it. Refer back to chapter 8 for assistance if necessary.

Practicing partner, you'll be asked to come up with a topic of conversation. Your partner will attempt to engage in the topic with you. Though your partner will be following prompts, go ahead and engage with them as is this were a real conversation. Like your partner, be mindful of the delivery of your messages.

Supporting partner, at your partner's cue, you may begin.

Tell me about something interesting or memorable that happened to you this week.

Supporting partner, really try to connect with the purpose of your partner's story. Share some initial thoughts you have, and be mindful of your delivery.

How do you feel about what happened?

Supporting partner, what's something you can say to validate your partner's experience?

Supporting partner, can you relate to your partner's topic with a personal example? If so, please share. If not, what else would you like to learn about their experience?

Supporting partner, what's something warm and positive you can say about what your partner shared? Here are some examples of things you can focus on:

- What does your partner's topic say about what's important to them?
- What does your partner's topic say about their values?
- Name something you admire about how they handled the situation.
- What's something you can compliment your partner on?

Both of the exercises in this section are designed to help the two of you foster a more positive atmosphere in your relationship through warm engagement. Couples who are warm with each other tend to feel more secure because the positive feelings produced by physical and verbal affection result in actively seeking to spend more time together. The more you practice warm interactions with each other, the more you'll choose to continue relating in this way, simply because it feels wonderful.

To continue this practice, show more positive affection toward each other, mind your manners, and speak to your partner like they are somebody you love. Never say to yourself, "They should know I love them," because there's value behind the added efforts you make to show them. If you need more help connecting with your partner in conversation, you can refer back to this exercise as a guide as often as you'd like.

In this chapter, you learned different ways to use your RQ skills to work through common relationship issues, and learned to work through difficulties to strengthen your relationship. Though it's ideal to have time to think through a problem before you approach your partner with it, you also have tools to manage in-the-moment difficulties by looking for ways to bring yourself and your partner back to emotional safety when things begin to escalate. The more conflicts you successfully overcome, the easier it'll be to navigate disagreements in the future. Of course, you'll still find yourselves in painful dispute from time to time, but those fights can also contribute to building resiliency, depending on how you handle it. In our last chapter together, you'll learn how to use RQ skills to get past an argument in order to further strengthen your relationship and deepen your intimacy.

Time for a Pause

Over the upcoming week, continue observing your relationship interactions with your partner and engaging each other with warmth. You've learned many RQ skills already throughout this book, and expecting to immediately apply them all, or even know where to use them, is not realistic. All you need to do is *try*. When there are moments of tension or unmet need, moments of disconnect, or even moments of connection, pay attention to the way you engage and be thoughtful about it. Here are some questions to ask yourself:

- Am I showing up in the best way here?
- What do I need in this moment?
- What does my partner need in this moment?
- What RQ skill do I want to practice more this week?
- What's an area of our relationship dynamics that I want to improve on?

CHAPTER 10

Using Relationship IQ Tools to Reconcile After a Fight

Each time you get into a fight with your partner, it shakes your relationship foundation even if just a bit. Maybe you've been there. In the heat of the moment, you and your partner exchange hurtful words, causing one or both of you to question your desires to continue the relationship. But not long after, your PNS kicks in to restore your logic, and you realize that you actually do want to be with this person. In those moments, all you want is to make things better, but you don't know how to get past the regretful things that were said or done.

Following a painful fight, couples often hurry to patch things up because the threat of emotional disconnection is too much to bear. While rushing to make up can restore an immediate sense of safety, not resolving the original source of conflict will leave your relationship vulnerable to more problems down the road and interfere with your long-term security. For true healing to occur after an emotional dispute, couples must actively engage each other in *reconciliation*, which is a mending process that helps them grow from conflict by gaining understanding of the factors that led to the conflict, and resolving the root issues. This contributes to a stronger sense of security for both partners—you're able to clear the obstacle in the way of connection and grow more confident in your relationship's ability to overcome challenges.

But there are many steps that must be taken before successful reconciliation and repair can take place, beginning with breaking silence after an argument. Let's take a look.

Breaking the Silence

After a big argument, it's normal and healthy to not talk for a period of time. Both partners need to remove themselves from the source of stress in order to restore a state of calm before the upsetting events can be processed. However, letting too much time pass can further agitate an already tense situation. This is why it's important to learn to break the silence in order to facilitate repair. Being the first to break the silence can be hard because of the vulnerable position you're in following an unsettling exchange. You're not sure how your partner will respond, and if they will reject your efforts.

You can start with assessing your readiness for repair. The best way to determine whether you're in the right emotional condition to talk is to know whether you're able to have empathy and compassion for your partner. Here are questions you might want to ask yourself.

Am I able to see my partner's perspective?

Am I at least ready to hear my partner's perspective?

What do I understand about my partner's intentions?

What part am I ready to take responsibility for in the argument?

How do I feel about my partner right now?

Once you've determined readiness to talk, you can test out your partner's readiness. Below are questions you can ask yourself to assess your partner's readiness for repair. Take turns answering the questions out loud to each other.

What are signs to you that your partner is *not* ready to be approached?

What are signs to you that your partner *is* ready to be approached?

Do you sometimes throw out little hints to your partner that you're ready to reconnect? If so, how do you do that?

The most difficult challenge to breaking the silence is being the first to initiate reconciliation. Especially when feelings are still raw, it's a lot to ask to put yourself in a vulnerable position to potentially be hurt again. You can make it easier on your partner by responding in a safe way. This doesn't mean you must be ready to patch things up when approached, but even when you're not ready to talk, you can still respond to them in a way that doesn't discourage them. Here are some things you can say to your partner if you're not ready for repair:

- "I appreciate you coming to me. I know how hard it was. Can we talk later? I'm still processing."
- "Thank you for taking the initiative. Can I come find you when I am ready to talk?"
- "I'm not ready to talk now, but I will come to you when I am."
- "I still need some more time to process my feelings, but thank you for letting me know that you're ready. I'll check in with you later."

How have the two of you broken the silence in the past? Take turns responding to these questions out loud in discussion format. Write down responses only where space is provided.

Who do you think more often takes initiative to break the silence?

What's the scariest thing about taking the initiative?

How does your partner usually respond when you take initiative?

What could your partner do to make it easier on you to take initiative?

What commitment can you make to your partner right now when they take the initiative in the future?

*Partner A:*____

____

*Partner B:*____

____

Though it seems simple, breaking the silence is typically the most difficult part of a repair effort. However, once the ice is broken, the sense of relief often makes it easier for you and your partner to be open in communication and listening. Let's take a look at the next step, making sense of the incident.

Making Sense of the Incident

Though these are not necessarily chronological steps to repair, making sense of the incident is a logical place to begin reconciliation. This is where you start to sort out what went wrong, gain clarity on each other's intentions, and take accountability for any hurtful words or actions carried out—sort of like putting together pieces of a puzzle. You might address the ways you went about the conversation, clear up any miscommunications or misperceptions, or directly address issues related to the conflict. By working through this step, you and your partner remove the obstacles keeping you from collaborative problem solving.

This exercise can walk you through the kinds of things you might address when you're working together to make sense of an incident. Both of you will work on this exercise together, and answer the same questions about the same incident. You will both decide to use *one* past argument to answer questions about, as if you're making sense of that experience in real-time. Read the questions out loud and take turns responding to them.

What's the past argument that you've both agreed to use for this exercise?

Use your feelings vocabulary to help your partner understand your perspective in this argument.

In your opinion, what went wrong?

What part of the conflict do you take responsibility for?

Explain what you were intending to do for the part you take responsibility for.

What were the consequences of your actions?

What do you understand about how you made your partner feel?

If you think your partner has miscommunicated or misunderstood something, clarify as needed.

What did you learn about your partner?

You may recall that many of those questions are similar to the steps you would take to making a sincere apology, which is part of gaining clarity. Once that's been achieved, you've prepared yourselves to resolve the original problem.

Resolving the Problem

Once you and your partner have learned more about what wasn't working, you can move on to exploring better ways of doing things. Here you can begin to narrow down the options for a plan to move forward. This is an important step because it reassures you and your partner that the original problem will no longer burden the relationship.

To demonstrate open-mindedness, the best way to approach finding a solution is when one partner invites the other to share ideas. The following exercise will walk you through what it could look like to find a resolution. Use the same incident from the previous exercise. Decide who will play which role, and swap roles when you're done.

Supporting partner, read the questions to your partner aloud. As you're listening to your partner, practice active listening skills.

What are some ideas you have to resolve this?

(What do you think about your partner's ideas? Don't hesitate to provide feedback if you have any. Can you provide some validation for what your partner wants?)

Specifically, what would you like me to do?

Supporting partner, this question is for you. Are you willing to do what your partner is asking? If not, what *are* you willing to do?

Once you've both had your opportunity to share your ideas about a possible solution, write down what you'll each do differently in the future:

*Partner A:*____

____

____

*Partner B:*____

____

____

Now that the two of you have a plan, the last but very important part of any repair effort is to reestablish connection.

Reestablishing Connection

Though simple, reestablishing connection is a very necessary step for both partners to feel secure again. Reestablishing connection is a deliberate action you take to mark the recommencement of intimacy. Arguments can be destabilizing, especially if things got heated and you may feel remorseful for certain things you've said or done. Reestablishing connection is how you and your partner reassure each other that your feelings have not changed, and that it's safe for the relationship to resume. It can be something as simple as asking for reassurance or indulging in a small treat like a trip to the ice-cream shop after dinner.

What do you do to reestablish connection? Engage each other in a brief discussion by taking turns responding to these questions.

How do you usually feel after a fight?

What have I said or done in the past that made you feel better after a fight?

What can I do to make you feel better after a fight?

Looks like we've come full circle in teaching you how to reestablish security. The goal of this last chapter was to give you the tools that you need to be fearless in your relationship. I hope that you're able to see that although arguments can be painful and upsetting, you never need to fear them. Each time you overcome an argument, it's another successful journey back to safety, and remember: safety is the gateway to security.

Conclusion

Congratulations, lovebirds. You've made it to the end, which is truly no small feat. The fact that you've stuck through it to this point proves that you're both invested in building a lasting future together. I want you to know that the mutual *desire* you both have to work on your relationship is the glue that's kept you together; all I was here to do was to take the guesswork out of having a good relationship.

Chances are, you both came into this journey with a lot of your own strengths as a couple, so don't feel as though you need to learn everything in this book to have a solid relationship. What's important here is that you recognize that healthy ways to approach difficult situations do exist, whether or not you choose to use them. Whatever you do choose to learn, be patient about it. As with learning anything new, it'll take time for the two of you to turn practice into habit, and even then, know that at times you will revert back to old behaviors.

You will continue to fight, to have moments of disconnection, to make decisions that unintentionally hurt each other, but those are all just opportunities to continue building your skills. With all of the hardships you get through together, the only thing that is expected to diminish over time is the question you have about whether you've chosen the right one for you.

If you haven't already realized in working through this book, there's nothing easy about building a strong relationship, and no matter where you are on your journey, the work *never* stops. Rather than being disappointed by that, I hope you feel inspired by knowing that all the efforts you put into your relationship only contribute to ever-expanding intimacy and to security that has no end.

Acknowledgments

As I sit here writing this, I'm overcome with gratitude. When I began this journey of writing my first book, I could never have imagined the kinds of challenges and growth that would come of it. I learned that writing a book was more than just lots and lots of research, writing, and organizing thoughts on paper. It was a team project that was supported by my closest friends, family, and colleagues, who all graciously filled the gaps left when I had to redirect my energies toward writing. There's literally no other way this book could've existed otherwise.

First and foremost, I thank my dad, Charles; mom, Laura; siblings Sandy, Cindy, Wendy, and Eric; their supportive spouses; and my nieces and nephews, Cara, Kyli, Wesley, and Max. You've all been the constant home I could go back to whenever I was craving comfort, joy, and safety.

I thank my husband, Antonio, for your undying patience and the sacrifices you made to support me through this challenging journey. I literally couldn't have completed this without you.

I thank my closest friends, Zora, Carolyn, and Ramichael, for giving me the space to be busy, and never making me feel like I'm not doing enough to deserve your loyalty.

To my psychology world: Sharissa, my work wife who's shown me that a business partnership is no different from a healthy marriage. My Flow & AT family, Ken, Julio, and Pat, who've been there through every phase of my psychology career and believed in me before I even started graduate studies. My therapist, Julie, who taught me self-compassion and made me truly believe in the power of psychological healing. My editors at New Harbinger, Ryan and Madison, who have been unbelievably patient and encouraging, and instilled in me the confidence I needed to keep going.

And to all my clients throughout the years who courageously shared your most vulnerable experiences with me, and gave me the opportunity to learn from you and become the psychologist I am today.

Betsy Chung, PsyD, is a licensed clinical psychologist in private practice in California. She was born and raised in Los Angeles, CA, to a culturally Chinese family. Currently, she is a relationship expert who splits her time between helping people strengthen their relationships in private practice, sharing her knowledge as a contributor to popular online media outlets, and serving as clinical director of Flow Wellness Hub—a holistic mental wellness practice in Huntington Beach, CA.

MORE BOOKS from NEW HARBINGER PUBLICATIONS

WIRED FOR LOVE, SECOND EDITION

How Understanding Your Partner's Brain and Attachment Style Can Help You Defuse Conflict and Build a Secure Relationship

978-1648482960 / US $19.95

SIMPLE WAYS TO UNWIND WITHOUT ALCOHOL

50 Tips to Drink Less and Enjoy More

978-1648482342 / US $18.95

ADULT DAUGHTERS OF NARCISSISTIC MOTHERS

Quiet the Critical Voice in Your Head, Heal Self-Doubt, and Live the Life You Deserve

978-1648480096 / US $18.95

HEALTHY CONFLICT, HAPPY COUPLE

How to Let Go of Blame and Grow Stronger Together

978-1648481697 / US $19.95

ACT WITH LOVE, SECOND EDITION

Stop Struggling, Reconcile Differences, and Strengthen Your Relationship with Acceptance and Commitment Therapy

978-1648481635 / US $19.95

WHEN A LOVED ONE WON'T SEEK MENTAL HEALTH TREATMENT

How to Promote Recovery and Reclaim Your Family's Well-Being

978-1648483134 / US $19.95

newharbingerpublications

1-800-748-6273 / newharbinger.com

(VISA, MC, AMEX / prices subject to change without notice)

Follow Us

Don't miss out on new books from New Harbinger.
Subscribe to our email list at **newharbinger.com/subscribe**